HARDBALL SELLING

How to Turn the Pressure On
Without Turning the Customer Off

— BY —

Robert L. Shook

REPLICA BOOKS

A DIVISION OF BAKER & TAYLOR
BRIDGEWATER, NJ

FIRST REPLICA BOOKS EDITION, MARCH 1998

Published by Replica Books, a division of Baker & Taylor,
1200 Route 22 East, Bridgewater, NJ 08807

Replica Books is a trademark of Baker & Taylor

Bibliographical Note

This Replica Books edition, first published in 1998, is an
unabridged republication of the work first published by
William Morrow and Company, Inc., New York, in 1991.

Manufactured in the United States of America

HARDBALL SELLING

HARDBALL SELLING
How to Turn the Pressure On
Without Turning Your Customer Off

ROBERT L. SHOOK

QUILL
WILLIAM MORROW
NEW YORK

To my sisters, Lois and Nancy,
with love

ACKNOWLEDGMENTS

I am grateful to the many wonderful men and women in the sales profession with whom I have been associated throughout my career, first as a salesperson, and later as a writer. The list is simply too long for me to include names, but, in particular, I was very fortunate to have a father who was a super salesperson, and who taught me the basics during my youthful, impressionable years. Through him, I learned that selling is a noble profession, and one that instills a sense of pride—but only when a professional approach is executed.

There are several people associated with the writing end of this book whom I also acknowledge for their fine efforts and assistance. Mary Liff, my secretary, did her usual good work in transcribing tapes, typing manuscript drafts, and organizing my filing system. Beverly Connor was helpful in the preparation of my first draft of the manuscript. And once the manuscript was completed and delivered to the publisher, Randy Ladenheim-Gil did a superb job as my editor. When Randy took a leave of absence to have her baby, Jennifer Ward and Andy Dutter took over and pinch-hit like all-star players, leaving me in awe of Morrow's impressive teamwork approach. I also appreciate my agent, Al Zuckerman, who played an important role. After all, he's the one who sold *Hardball* to the publisher.

CONTENTS

INTRODUCTION

"Off the record ..."

I am well aware that high-pressure selling is scorned by the American consumer, so I don't anticipate receiving accolades for authoring this book. In fact, those who read only the title on the book jacket are apt to be turned off, and certainly many book reviewers with no sales experience may be offended.

This negative reaction should come as no surprise to anyone who sells for his or her livelihood. America has never held its immense corps of salespeople in high esteem. The poor image traces back to the days of the snake oil pitchmen, when deceptive practices used to coerce people into buying needless and overpriced merchandise were the norm. It took a strong and sustained public outcry to force salespeople to clean up their act. Of course, there will always be some snake oil pitchman types out there fleecing and alienating the public. But these are the exception now, not the rule. The majority of salespeople are sincere and trustworthy, but now the pendulum has swung too far. Today's breed of salespeople are courteous but far too cautious. They have allowed the customer to take charge. This recent stereotype has provided the American buyer with a new whipping boy.

I am all for common courtesy. However, there is a point when being too cordial is just that: *too* cordial. It creates an atmosphere conducive only to procrastination. Making it easy for someone to say no is counterproductive. And counterproductivity means no sale. A salesperson must remember that *nothing happens until a sale is made.* The objective is to close a sale and maintain a high level of customer satisfaction. It takes a no-nonsense approach to accomplish this in today's competitive business world. There is no place for passivity. Bear in mind the adage: "A successful person learns all the rules and follows them to the letter. A supersuccessful person learns all the rules, and then breaks them, when necessary, one by one."

I challenge you: Dare to be different. Start by accepting the fact that you will never be a leading sales producer by imitating the threadbare methods that America's salespeople have been practicing for more than a half century. Raise your level of expectation several notches. Mediocrity will not suffice. What does it take to stand out from the crowd? It takes making demands and meeting demands, and a tough-minded and single-purpose stance. Under many circumstances, *I endorse high-pressure selling.* Unfortunately, most salespeople have been brainwashed. They have little understanding of the positive role high pressure can play in closing sales. High-pressure selling generally connotes images of salespeople browbeating defenseless customers. Understandably, these tactics are frowned upon by both buyer and seller.

Don't be too quick to judge my position on high-pressure selling. I don't condone mistreating customers and I despise misrepresentation. There is no place for such behavior in the field of professional selling. There is a subtle form of high-pressure selling, however, that I don't find offensive. Inoffensive high-pressure selling must be delicately executed—no buyer consciously wants to be pressured. It's the ability to close a sale *after* the prospect has expressed his disinterest to buy that separates the top producers from the masses of commonplace salespeople. In fact, a high percentage of sales made by superior salespeople come after an intention not to buy has been expressed at least once. These are "borderline" cases—sales that could go either way but are closed with some *extra persuasion.* Often the right application of high-pressure selling is vital and without it, many sales presentations suffer a sudden and premature death. The conversion of these "near hits" to closed sales is the difference between mediocrity and superiority in the sales field.

I am about to shatter certain myths about high-pressure selling. For instance, high-pressure salespeople and fast-buck artists are not synonymous. Nor should anyone who employs high-pressure selling techniques be viewed automatically as someone using underhanded selling methods or engaging in unfair competition practices. The fact is, high-pressure selling can be perfectly compatible with professionalism and having the customer's best interest at heart.

I urge you to read this book with an open mind. Nothing contained herein suggests you should compromise your integrity or conduct yourself in any way that is detrimental to the buyer. On the contrary, you will discover that by selling according to the concepts and principles I describe, both seller and buyer benefit.

Hardball: High-Pressure Selling Techniques That Work has an essential message for every salesperson; it offers lessons that are vital for anyone seeking success in his or her sales career. This is not another garden-variety book about selling. The marketplace is saturated with how-to books that, for the most part, differ from each other only in writing style, not content. There is no reason for me to add yet another such book to an already long and undistinguished list. My objective is to produce something of substance that is significantly different. What you will find in *Hardball* is not imparted in other sales books. You are about to gain new insights into selling that may be controversial, but I know my method works. While you may not agree with it in its entirety, I guarantee that my message will be enlightening.

While I have authored twenty-five books, my business background covers seventeen years as a full-time salesman and sales manager. For the record, I write about my subject with authority. If it sounds like I'm tooting my own horn, I am, but only to emphasize an important point. I have a strong track record in sales, coupled with having spent thousands of hours with the world's best salespeople. I have written about these successful sellers, and I have coauthored books with the top sales leaders in the automotive, computer, insurance, real estate, and securities fields. I have been out there in the trenches with them, observing them on the firing line. This kind of exposure gives me a unique background.

Hardball draws upon my close contacts with these sales leaders, a phenomenal resource virtually untapped by other writers. A major portion of the material contained in this book was originally collected from countless hours of tape-recorded interviews. I am revealing here things told to me that have never appeared in my previous books. These "off the record" comments are the *real* advice you need but won't read about elsewhere or hear at seminars.

I'm sure, therefore, that you will understand why I can't always use real names in this book. My no-name policy honors all off-the-record requests. Don't get the idea that there's anything deceptive or dishonorable about the sales concepts and techniques that are routinely *not* quoted when the world's great salespeople discuss their secrets. Their intent is not to shortchange you. Instead they are concerned about being quoted out of context and consequently appearing to be manipulative and offensive. Projecting such an image would jeopardize the relationships they have established with their customers, in particular those with whom they are currently conducting business. But the names themselves are not important. It's what you can learn from what these supersalespeople do that matters.

Successful selling is a matter of recognizing the thin line that exists between an industry sales leader and the rest of the pack. This line can be quite subtle, but it marks the split between winners and losers. Admittedly, on the surface, this fine line seems somewhat insignificant, but be on notice that it can make the difference between attaining mediocrity and enormous success as a salesperson. And anything that can possibly have such an impact on your life is, at the very least, something deserving of your serious attention. So read carefully, for what I will convey to you in detail throughout the pages of *Hardball* is how to make hardball selling work for you.

1

The Hardball Philosophy

The mere mention of high-pressure selling can antagonize people. Yet, I am willing to take the heat for writing *Hardball* because it contains a philosophy that needs to be told to the millions of men and women whose livelihoods depend on closing sales.

Over the years I've observed that one's overall success in selling is not solely dependent upon how well he presents his product. Eventually, the vast majority of salespeople can adequately explain the merits of their products. However, more is required than simply providing an explanation or giving a demonstration of one's product; a videocassette or even a well-written brochure can accomplish that. While a prospect must feel the need for a product, he or she must also be motivated to buy it.

For years, we have heard sales managers throughout the U.S. say that the top 20 percent of their sales force generates 80 percent of their sales volume. This is a revealing statistic. It means that the top salespeople are producing at a rate sixteen times greater than the rest. This truth underscores how vital it is to be among the ranks of this top echelon because run-of-the-mill salespeople are barely making ends meet. With only a one-in-five likelihood of making it in the high-production group, settling for mediocrity is unthinkable. You must strive for excellence or seek another career.

The Four Principles of Hardball Selling

To accept the concept of hardball selling, you must understand the following four principles:

Number One—*The Tendency to Procrastinate.* When given a choice, a prospect will delay making a buying decision.

Number Two—*Nobody Wants to Procrastinate.* While a prospect may choose to delay making a buying decision, he or she does not *like* to procrastinate.

Number Three—*The Need to Apply High Pressure.* A prospect may need to be high-pressured, yet he or she will resist it.

Number Four—*High Pressure Works Best When It's Subtle.* Because a prospect will resist high pressure, its application must be subtle in order to be inoffensive.

You must fully comprehend and accept these four principles in order to succeed as a hardball salesperson. One hundred percent acceptance is required; anything less is inadequate.

These principles evolved over a quarter of a century and are based on a combination of my personal selling experiences, extensive interviews that I conducted with the world's leading salespeople, and observations I have made of them during actual sales presentations. You are advised to study these principles and learn them. Then, practice them until they become second nature.

The Tendency to Procrastinate

Most people have difficulty making decisions to buy, especially when they're out of their area of expertise. The less extensive one's knowledge, the more he or she will tend to procrastinate. For instance, a neurosurgeon or a heart surgeon must make life-or-death, split-second decisions in the operating theater. As Denton Cooley, the renowned Houston heart surgeon, explains: "In open-heart surgery, there is so little time available to get the job done. Even these mechanical devices we use to support life while we're operating can give us only a limited amount of time. So, the slightest hesitation ... the failure to make a quick decision ... a quivering hand ... any of these can cause irrevocable damage. In other words, a lack of confidence can be fatal." Even individuals such as Cooley who perform so decisively in their area of expertise may be hesitant about signing an order form to purchase an automobile or a personal computer, and a real estate developer or securities analyst may agonize when purchasing seemingly trivial items such as a tie, or a bottle of perfume.

It's also true that buying decisions that involve a lot of money increase one's tendency to procrastinate. While someone may easily make a quick decision to purchase office supplies, he would probably act less decisively when purchasing a large-scale computer system for his business.

The combination of making a decision concerning an unfamiliar and expensive product compounds the tendency to procrastinate. It would be tough, for instance, to sell a case of highly expensive wine to someone who knew nothing about fine wines. So would the sale of a costly diamond ring to someone unfamiliar with the values and quality of precious gems.

Rather than risking getting hurt, the potential purchaser will try to take the easy way out and delay his decision-making.

Because the tendency to procrastinate is based on either confusion or fear of making an expensive mistake, it is the salesman's fault if a sale is lost to procrastination. In the former case, generally the salesperson has failed to fully educate the buyer. In the latter, the fear is based on a prospect's concern that a wrong decision could be a source of embarrassment as well as financial loss; it's the salesman's responsibility to reassure the client as to the wisdom of each purchase.

Nobody Wants to Procrastinate

In the Aesop fable about Buridan's Ass, the ass starves himself to death while standing between two stacks of hay, unable to decide which is the more desirable to eat. Too often, I believe, salespeople put prospects in a similar position by allowing them to avoid decisions. Nobody wants to procrastinate. Indecision is frustrating.

A prospect prefers to be decisive, and when he has a need for your product and doesn't buy, he experiences discomfort or anxiety or both. People don't want to experience these disagreeable emotions. They are annoyed at a salesperson, who, after explaining the benefits of his product, doesn't adequately create a need for owning it. Failing to close the sales robs the client of the satisfactory completion of the buying process.

The Need to Apply High Pressure

People have a natural tendency to procrastinate but don't like it; your job as a salesperson is to motivate them to make a buying decision. Your success in selling rests on your ability to overcome procrastination. While clients may express their desire to postpone a buying decision, and are frustrated by their indecision, *they don't want you to apply high pressure.* It can appear to be a damned-if-you-do, damned-if-you-don't situation. Actually, it's only damned if you don't. Whenever I face this dilemma I elect to apply high pressure because it's a reliable way to get a reaction. Rarely do people simply straddle the fence afterward. They know I mean business.

Since I wholeheartedly believe in my product and recognize the ways in which it will benefit my prospect, my prime objective during a sales presentation is to motivate him to own it. At the same time, I have a clear understanding why he has a tendency to procrastinate, and I recognize that it bothers him. Knowing this, I am cognizant that my job is to get him off dead center; if I don't accomplish this, I've failed to do my job properly. My mission is to convince him that by delaying a buying decision, he will suffer an adverse consequence. When high pressure is necessary to get the job done, I never hesitate to use it. I do this knowing that when a prospect truly needs my product, both of us benefit from my ability to convince him to make a buying decision. I'm willing to risk applying high pressure in this situation even though I'm aware that I may ruffle some feathers in the process. The fact that prospects don't like high-pressure selling is no excuse to back off. Even in a worst-case scenario, when its use might cause a presentation to come to an abrupt halt, a hardball salesperson must not relent. While the easy way is to take the path of least resistance and back off, it is also the cowardly way—in spite of the ensuing consequences. That's why I call it playing hardball. It's not always the most pleasant way to sell, but it does get the best results.

High Pressure Works Best When It's Subtle

The following is a summary of the first three hardball principles in a single sentence: People tend to procrastinate but they don't like to, so high pressure must be applied to close the sale.

If it's not perfectly clear and acceptable to you, I recommend that you review these first three principles before reading the final and most important one.

Because nobody likes being high-pressured, your execution must be subtle; if not, it won't work. The key to successful hardball selling rests on the fourth principle: *High pressure works best if it's subtle.* Excel at high-pressure selling and prospects will be unaware that you're doing it. Hence, they won't be offended.

One thing is certain: High-pressure selling is most offensive when it's obvious to the buyer. Only a masochist enjoys feeling manipulated or intimidated. And when high pressure is applied improperly, this is exactly how a prospect feels. The secret is to be so proficient at high-pressure selling that it goes undetected. To successfully walk this tightrope requires an awareness (which you now have) and a complete understanding of the way it works. The better you are at it, the less obvious it is. To attain a high level of competence takes hard work. This book is dedicated to your achieving a respectable degree of proficiency.

A Convincing Case for Hardball Selling

Early in my sales management career in the insurance field, I received a telephone call from an attorney with the investigating division of the Ohio Department of Insurance. He wanted to discuss a "problem" involving one of my new agents whom I had personally trained. We met the next morning.

"We've had three callers complaining that your agent used high-pressure tactics," he told me in an authoritative voice, "and we don't tolerate that sort of behavior."

"I understand how you feel," I said, "but as we both know, a new agent is not always likely to find many welcome mats when he's out there pounding the pavement. Most people resist insurance agents because buying what they know their families desperately need means facing their own mortality. They would rather procrastinate, and my agent knows that if he doesn't close a sale at the time of his presentation, the chances of doing so become slimmer as time passes."

"I know all of that," he snapped at me. "Now I haven't got all day. What exactly is your point?"

"My point is that if pressure isn't exerted when it's needed, a salesperson is going to fall flat on his face. As you know, every top insurance agent uses some high-pressure tactics, but when he's good at it, people don't notice it, and complaints aren't registered.

"My agent is just a rookie and he simply hasn't developed the skill to delicately high-pressure anyone. That's not his fault: It's mine. Evidently, I didn't train him well enough. Therefore, what I plan to do is train him to be so good at high-pressure selling that you'll never receive another complaint about him. Meanwhile, please be patient. He'll require some time to become proficient."

The attorney understood. My agent got the time he needed, the attorney bought me lunch, and my respect for state bureaucrats increased.

The Law of Diminishing Returns

The application of hardball selling techniques necessitates a complete understanding of *the law of diminishing returns.* The following analogy illustrates how this law works.

Jack hasn't eaten for the entire day. When he's given a delicious apple he quickly devours it with immense pleasure. He's given a second apple and, still hungry, he eats and enjoys this one too—but not to the same extent as he did the first apple. His hunger already satisfied, Jack is given yet another apple, which he eats reluctantly, and with some displeasure. Although Jack has no desire to eat more apples, he's ordered to eat another one, and with each bite, he becomes more and more nauseous. He receives less pleasure, and he becomes sicker with each succeeding apple.

Just as Jack's appetite progressively decreased, the law of diminishing returns has the same effect on the close of a sale. A prospect has the most enthusiasm to own your product at the end of your sales presentation, because you have just created the need for it. If a buying decision is delayed because the prospect wants to think it over, the more time that lapses, the more input he gets from competitors, the more doubts arise, the less chance you have of closing the sale. The prospect retains less and less information about why he should buy your product; at the same time, he begins to think more about how his money might be better spent on something else, or not spent at all. In short, he cools off.

Along with having a thorough understanding of the law of diminishing returns, you must be willing to risk applying high pressure to close the sale at the time of the first presentation or accept the fact that it will probably never happen. Because the odds for success are in favor of closing the sale during the initial presentation and dramatically decrease with the passage of time, "borderline" sales that could go either way are lost when salespeople fail to go for a closing at once and instead consent to call again at the prospect's convenience for a delayed decision. Some sales might have materialized through a callback, and you must expect to lose some due to high pressure, but in the long run you probably will gain many more. You should never attempt to decide *which* prospects may be sold by opting to make a callback. It simply isn't possible to single out the "probable" ones, barring being blessed with some divine telepathic powers. So, rather than leaving it to guesswork, don't even attempt to single out the probable ones. Instead, I urge you to execute your close on these borderline prospects. By doing so, you are certain to realize a dramatic rise in your sales production, and as a direct consequence, your earnings will similarly increase.

A Nonadversary Relationship

People often believe that high-pressure selling is synonymous with twisting somebody's arm to sign an order form, coupled with selling a bill of goods of little or no value. Contrary to the consensus in the U.S., high-pressure selling can be compatible with caring for others and acting in the customer's best interest. It's the snake-oil-salesman, a-sucker-is-born-every-minute image that's working against you. That sales approach is unconscionable, but just because an idea or technique has been abused by unethical people, it is not necessarily an evil in itself. High-pressure selling can work for or against the prospect, depending on its application.

I'm not so naive as to be blind to the fact that there are high-pressure salespeople in this world who wouldn't hesitate to sell their firstborn in exchange for a quick buck. These shysters are despicable and should be recognized as such. Yet, I believe properly applied high pressure is commendable and should be used. It's important to realize that two brands of high-pressure selling exist; you must be wise enough to recognize the ways in which they differ.

In a successful seller-buyer relationship, there must be harmony. The salesperson's reason for being is to provide service to the customer. Ideally, a teamwork effort exists, a "we" relationship rather than an "us versus them" relationship.

Hardball selling must be accompanied by a nurturing attitude. The good news is that a hardball salesperson can take a firm stance, be single-minded in his objective to close the sale, and simultaneously serve the customer. This is the way it's supposed to be!

When a prospect is aware that you are, indeed, acting in his best interests, it is unlikely that he will resist high-pressure efforts meant to convince him to make an on-the-spot buying decision. But note that you must also have conviction in your product, which is bound to be noticed by the buyer. Without a caring attitude and conviction, hardball selling is ineffective.

A life insurance agent who truly believes that a prospect's family must be financially protected would be performing a disservice by backing off in response to a procrastinator's request to delay his buying decision. This is particularly true when the agent knows from prior experience that there's little chance of closing the sale after the prospect has been permitted to "take his time and sleep on it."

Likewise, a real estate broker must exert pressure to sell a starter house to a young couple who has been house-hunting for more than a year. They might say, "We've been looking to buy a house, but we never seem to be able to make a decision to purchase one." The broker knows a "hot" house will sell quickly; by allowing the couple to procrastinate, they are likely to lose the opportunity to buy what is ideal for them.

A computer salesperson realizes that a small bank must computerize its customer service department if it wants to offer competitive banking services. "Yes, I suppose we're going to make the transition someday," a sleepy bank president explains, "but in the past, we've always conducted our business without a computer, and somehow we've managed so far." In this case the salesperson knows that his job is cut out for him to convince the banker to act now. If a buying decision is postponed, the banker will continue to delay installing a computer system and as a result, the bank will continue to lose customers. This is a case in which a salesperson must prod the customer to buy his product for his own good.

Yet another situation where some high pressure is necessary is a case involving an elderly couple who keeps procrastinating over a decision to buy a condominium in Florida. "I know money isn't an issue," the salesman says, "but it's too bad that in your efforts to be good parents and grandparents, you have denied yourselves many fine things you are entitled to enjoy. I can assure you that you have no reason to feel guilty about buying something for *you.* You deserve it. But if you don't buy a condo now, in all probability you never will. The time has come for you to enjoy the good life before it's too late." This hardball salesman has expressed himself well; by his application of high pressure, the elderly couple might make a decision that is right for them that they would never have made otherwise.

An even more striking example of how high-pressure selling serves the best interest of the other party is when a cancer patient is told that immediate surgery for the removal of a malignant breast tumor is essential. The woman may protest and claim to want several more opinions before having a mastectomy, but the physician knows that the longer she delays her (buying) decision, the worse is her prognosis for a full recovery. "Get a second opinion but do it quickly. The best time for your surgery is now," he persists, "and each day that you delay your decision about surgery, the more you place your life in jeopardy." It's evident here how essential it is that a salesperson (or doctor) has a clear understanding about the law of diminishing returns. At the very least, it's apparent that the doctor's high-pressure selling skills are truly necessary to help the patient make the right decision. It's fortunate that life-or-death decisions aren't in the hands of the typical salesperson! It's one matter when a sale dies, but it's catastrophic to lose a patient as a consequence of inability to close a sale.

In the above scenarios, a salesperson has an obligation to motivate the prospect into making a buying decision. By failing to do so, the prospect is exposed to the possibility of suffering a loss. When a salesperson shies away from exerting high pressure out of fear of creating animosity, no matter how unintentional, the prospect suffers. Under these circumstances, lacking the skills to close a sale is unprofessional and clearly detrimental to the buyer. Every salesperson has an obligation to be proficient, and to be otherwise makes him guilty of failing to act in his customer's best interest. There is no place in today's selling world for anyone who is too timid to provide his clients with obvious and beneficial solutions.

Helping the Buyer Make the Right Decision

"What gives you the right to decide what is in the prospect's best interest?" people ask. "It should be up to the prospect to make his own buying decision."

The final decision *is*, of course, the client's, but as a hardball salesperson, you have the obligation to advise, guide, and pressure prospects to do what is best for them. That's what a sales expert is trained to do; that's how a highly paid commissioned salesperson earns his keep.

Just as an attorney or consultant has a responsibility to steer his client in the right direction, so must a professional salesperson guide his prospect. If you truly are an expert in your field (a prerequisite for a hardball salesperson), it's also probable that you know better than your client if purchasing your product is in his best interest. If you sincerely believe that the prospect will be better off owning your product, in all probability, he will. Realizing that procrastination is potentially harmful, you can best serve your customer by not allowing him to postpone making the right buying decision.

Success Does Not Depend on a Single Sale

In the beginning of my career, I subjected myself to unnecessary stress by placing too much importance on every call I made. This made me overly cautious, and I hesitated to apply high pressure out of fear of antagonizing someone. Working as a straight commission salesman also pressed me to sell conservatively because it hurt my wallet when a sale didn't materialize.

I eventually overcame my fear by convincing myself that no single prospect would make or break me—no particular prospect meant so much that my career would be placed in jeopardy if I lost that one sale. We live in a big country and it's an even bigger world—and we live in an era where we have a world marketplace. There are so many prospects on our planet that it's impossible to run out of them. No matter how many sales you *don't* make, there are always opportunities to sell to someone else. Imagine, for example, how many calls a stockbroker would have to make before running out of prospects. In a thousand years of working 'round the clock, twenty-four hours a day, he could exhaust but a small fraction of the potential investors in the U.S. *Every* salesperson has an unlimited number of potential clients.

Once you relieve yourself of the worry about losing a sale, you will sell more effectively because you aren't "selling scared." When you waver during the close the prospect will mimic you psychologically, and be indecisive. Conversely, when you ask for the order with confidence, the prospect reacts with confidence, and he, too, will be decisive. And remember: The less pressure you put on yourself, the more you can exert on your prospect.

I sold my first few books to publishers without the aid of an agent. I did this not because I had no need for an agent, but because I was unable to obtain a good one. At a particular meeting with a major New York publishing house, I arrived a few minutes early, but the editor kept me waiting for nearly an hour before inviting me into his office.

No apology was made for the delay; instead, he said: "I have a workload you would not believe, Shook, so you should realize that you're very fortunate that I've agreed to see you today. Now, you've got five minutes to tell me about your manuscript, which, frankly, I don't think is right for us."

Five minutes! I thought to myself. This was supposed to be a half-hour meeting.

As I was about to speak, the editor's secretary entered the room. "Sir, your call from Mr. Forter is on line one. Should I tell him you're in conference?"

"I'll take it," he replied. "Frank," he shouted into the phone, "you son of a bitch, what the hell are you trying to do to us?"

Sensing this might be a personal call, I stood up to leave, but the editor nodded for me to sit down. "You dumb bastard," he screamed into the phone. "There is no goddamn way I will agree to those terms..."

For fifteen minutes he shouted four-letter obscenities, while I sat opposite him. Then he abruptly slammed down the receiver and exclaimed, "I'll nail that mother, if it's the last thing I ever do!" He then turned to me and said, "I have a meeting and I'm running late, so you now have sixty seconds to talk. Or if you'd rather, we can reschedule the meeting for sometime tomorrow."

I stood up and said, "I'm sorry, but you're not someone with whom I'll consider doing business."

"What do you mean?" he said with a surprised expression on his face.

"Let me put it to you this way," I answered. "If you were the last publisher in the world, and I had the last manuscript in the world, it would mean the end of the publishing business." I walked out of his office feeling very good about myself.

Now this does not imply that I'm advising you to avoid situations when you encounter confrontation, or, for that matter, a difficult prospect who, right off the bat, gives you a hard time. My decision not to do business with this particular individual was primarily based on how rudely he spoke to the telephone caller. Furthermore, we had scheduled a half-hour meeting, which he reduced to five minutes, and then to one minute! I realized that there was little I could accomplish by attempting to sell my manuscript in a sixty-second time frame. And I felt he lacked integrity for failing to honor his commitment by not seeing me for the full half hour (barring an emergency or an unavoidable occurrence, a businessperson should never renege on a scheduled meeting). What's more, it is essential for an author and editor to have a special rapport—if one does not exist, the publishing of the manuscript will fail to reach its full potential. So, under these circumstances, I felt justified in politely telling him off, and, in the process, saving my self-esteem. There were hundreds of other editors in New York, and I was certain one of them would buy my manuscript! Life is simply too short to deal with people who cause a lot of unnecessary grief.

Tenacity

There are always those hard-nosed prospects who will stubbornly resist any efforts you make to close the sale. They will throw every objection in the book at you and offer an array of reasons why you should call back later for their decision. You must realize that it's the nature of some people to resist, and despite the hassle, you must persist. To paraphrase Winston Churchill, "Never give in ... never, never, never." It has never been said that every sale is an easy sale—some prospects require more of a selling effort than others. You can't afford to walk away from these prospects; they represent potential sales production which, with tenacity, can materialize. Often, the harder a sale is to close, the better it will stick on the books.

So persevere. Stay in there and don't give up without a fight. As the great football coach Woody Hayes once said, "It is not the dog in the fight that matters, but rather it's the fight in the dog." As in an athletic event, it's often that extra effort that brings victory; a salesperson must possess the same driving tenacity.

A Total Acceptance of the Hardball Philosophy

To sell hardball, you must accept this philosophy 100 percent. Anything less will have little or no impact on your career.

Hardball selling has a bedrock philosophy which advocates that when it's time to close the sale, you must take a firm, *now-or-never* stance. It dictates that you frequently exert high pressure or risk losing the sale altogether. As a percentage player, you are always fully aware that the odds are heavily stacked in your favor and you *must* go with the odds.

There is no such thing as a half-hearted hardball salesman. You can't go through the motions, and, on occasion, employ hardball selling. Those salespeople who, on a whim, exert high pressure are seldom good at it, and most generally fall flat on their faces. A watered-down effort is easily sensed by prospects, and as a result has no effect. This means that you must never allow a single client to offer a lame excuse for not buying. Commit yourself to this hardball philosophy and never deviate from it.

Being Programmed to Close the Sale

Once you are 100 percent committed to the hardball philosophy, everything you do during your sales presentation will be geared to closing the sale. This orientation will begin from the moment you approach the office receptionist and continue throughout the sale. With single-minded momentum, you will be *programmed* to make every sale. All bridges will have been burned behind you. There is no other alternative except to close every sale. Nothing else is acceptable! Callbacks are unthinkable.

Once your subconscious is programmed with the hardball philosophy, it's as if a little voice is constantly guiding you to move in the right direction. Each time you stray from it, the little voice tells you, "Don't do that. That will hurt your effort to close the sale. Do this! This will help you." Soon you'll be on "automatic pilot," always doing what must be done to achieve your objective. When this happens, I assure you that it's a wonderful feeling. Your customers will "feel" your confidence and buy your product. What's more, they won't feel the least bit of high pressure; when they make the decision to buy, it will seem like an "automatic" response to your sales presentation.

In interviews with top salespeople, I always ask the question: "When do you assume the sale?" The reply is always the same: "I assume it from the moment the sales presentation begins."

To these top sellers, it's a natural expectation: "Why else would anyone agree to listen to a sales presentation?" If an interest is there, a sale should be assumed. For example, a good automobile salesperson thinks: "Anyone who walks into the showroom is obviously interested in purchasing a car. Why else would he come in?" A real estate broker assumes the sale because a prospect is house-shopping, and an insurance agent assumes a prospect is interested in buying a life insurance policy when he agrees to listen to the sales presentation. When a salesperson assumes the sale from the initial contact with the prospect an ideal atmosphere in which to buy is created. Conversely, when a salesperson is consumed with doubt and hesitates he faces a constant uphill battle.

I have observed many of the world's greatest salespeople, and each of them is self-programmed in this manner. For the most part, they are not even aware of what makes them so effective; they have difficulty explaining their success. Those who are self-programmed to close sales don't find it necessary to know why they are extraordinarily successful; anyone who's not will find it is essential to learn.

2

Getting Your Foot in the Door

It shouldn't come as a surprise to anyone that getting your foot in the door is a prerequisite for making a sale. And like most things in life there's a right way and a wrong way to make your approach.

It's true that first impressions are lasting ones. Your initial contact with a prospect has a profound influence on closing the sale because it's then that the mood is set for the entire presentation. Should the prospect initially identify you as a meek salesperson, it's unlikely that his perception will reverse during the course of your visit. I don't want you to think that a mild-mannered approach could evolve into an effective close: It doesn't happen that way in the real world of selling, and I'm offended when people imply that it does.

For example, I recently bristled while reading a book that told about a salesman who, after a thirty-minute wait to see a prospect, said to the receptionist, "Would you please tell Mr. Smith that it's okay that he can't see me. But I want you to ask him to please return my business card to me."

When the receptionist conveyed this message, her boss picked up the card and said, "What's so unusual about this card? Wait . . . let me examine it." Then the humor dawned on him and he grinned. "Send that salesman in immediately. I want to talk to anyone who is that imaginative."

Imagination, my foot. The salesman behaved like a scared rabbit. "It's preposterous for the author to refer to this episode as "sales magic." The salesperson might as well have said, "He probably doesn't want to buy anything today, does he?"

It's difficult for me to imagine a mealy-mouthed approach resulting in a successful sales interview. In the real world of selling, a timid approach rarely if ever works, and with such a high failure rate, it's wrong to pass along harmful advice to anyone whose livelihood is dependent on his or her sales production.

It even galls me to hear a salesperson say, "I'd like to come by and share an idea with you." The word *share* has been worked to death for years! There was a time when I liked it, but then everyone started *sharing,* and it lost its punch. After all, no salesman in his right mind would consider introducing himself: "Hi, I'm a typical salesman." Yet, this is exactly what happens when you approach prospects with the same spiel as scores of other salespeople. While you might not use the words to identify yourself as an ordinary peddler, that's the message that comes across loud and clear.

Know Thy Gatekeeper

Often clients use receptionists, secretaries, and assistants in a position I refer to as "gatekeeper." As a general rule, the more the boss values his or her time—and this includes a majority of the most affluent prospects—the more he or she is likely to be shielded by a gatekeeper. This individual is responsible for screening calls because the prospect doesn't have enough time to see every salesperson. On occasion it's essential, however, to hear out some salespeople. Accordingly, it's the gatekeeper's job to select the suitable from the masses. While this may be a job designated to a gatekeeper, it's *your* job to get past the gate. Not just now and then, but regularly.

It's less difficult to get past the gatekeeper than to secure an appointment with a prospect who doesn't employ someone for gate control. This is true because the gatekeeper neither makes buying decisions nor takes money out of his or her pocket when a sale is consummated. Furthermore, this person is unlikely to be in upper management, so you're not dealing with a "heavy." It is therefore decidedly less difficult to lock horns with a gatekeeper than with the actual buyer.

Yet, because the prospect respects the judgment of a gatekeeper, he's more apt to lower his guard and hear out those salespersons who do manage to enter his sanctuary. Knowing this, you should welcome the opportunity to meet head-on with gatekeepers; if you approach them properly, they're your ticket into the prospects' chambers.

Gatekeepers don't like being hassled, nor do they particularly relish being on the receiving end of a hardball sales pitch. "I'm not paid enough money to endure this kind of grief," they complain. They would rather dispatch hardball salespeople directly to the big cheese and let him take the heat. After all, the easy way out is for them to avoid confrontation. In my years of experience in dealing with gatekeepers, I have observed that they don't like to lock horns with a hardball salesperson. They have no problem, however, giving the walking papers to a meek salesperson.

My First Hardball Approach

As a young man just beginning my sales career, I soon discovered that I was getting nowhere with a friendly "Good-morning, I'm-Bob-Shook-and-here's-my-business-card-and-I'd-like-to-see-Mr. Beaver." While the books on selling and my sales manager advocated being cheerful and submissive, I was rarely greeted with open arms.

"How could so many people be so harsh and unresponsive to an eager, wholesome young person?" I wondered. In retrospect, I know how naive I was.

My stomach would churn as I waited in reception areas while other salespeople scooted past gatekeepers, often taking *my* appointment, leaving me with no recourse but to wait. Precious minutes slowly turned into hours. I studied the successful salespeople and, over a period of time, made several observations. First, they neither represented a better company nor sold a superior product. Second, my lack of success wasn't because I was young and inexperienced; some of them were my own age. The more I studied them, the more I became convinced that there was a certain intangible common denominator that these sellers shared.

In time, I discovered the secret ingredient. *It was their attitude.* The supersellers walked in as if they owned the place. They radiated self-confidence. Once I observed a particular man who made a strong impression on me. "He reminds me of somebody I know," I kept saying to myself. Suddenly it dawned on me: "John Wayne. He even has the Duke's swagger." I began to daydream about certain Hollywood heroes—Clark Gable, Humphrey Bogart, and Gary Cooper—imagining each of them making sales calls. It blew my mind to visualize Coop's facial expressions and body language. I pictured him being escorted directly into the prospect's office, having hardly said a word.

I became so excited that I could hardly wait to try out my theory. Knowing I had already blown this call, I was ready to conduct a cold-call experiment with a prospect down the street. This time I was set on doing it Gary Cooper style. I carefully pictured him in my mind as I approached the receptionist. Like Coop, I *knew* I was going to get in to see the prospect.

"The name is Shook," I said slowly. "Robert Shook." After a long pause, I continued. "Would you tell Mr. Hyatt that I'm here to see him."

"What company are you with?"

"The name is Shook, and I'm with Shook Associates," I repeated. "Would you tell Mr. Hyatt that I'm here?"

I stared right into her eyes, and without saying another word, she walked into Hyatt's office.

"Shook? Who is he?" I heard him ask.

"He's with Shook Associates, and it seems important," she said.

Hyatt came out. I told him, "Let's go into your office where we can talk in private."

"I'm sorry," he replied, as if having reason to apologize. "Yes, won't you please come into my office, Mr. Shook?"

Projecting a Winning Image

Analyzing what occurred, I concluded that my image had as much to do with getting my foot in the door as what I had said. Visualizing myself as Gary Cooper did wonders for my self-esteem. I walked in feeling good about myself. Confidence was written all over my face; I was glowing with the stuff. It showed in the manner in which I walked, or should I say, swaggered. As books are judged by their covers, so do prospects quickly decide whom to hear out and whom to throw out.

As I gained more experience, other successes followed. I kept polishing up my act, constantly making small improvements. I learned everything from what is the right clothing to which is the appropriate hairstyle. Each added touch by itself seemed relatively unimportant, but the total package had *success* written all over it.

Today I firmly believe that the salesperson who projects a professional and *prosperous* image stacks the cards greatly in his favor during this crucial first phase of the selling process. I'm convinced that businesspeople who place a premium on their time often make snap decisions about which salespeople to allow through the door. All things considered, they're influenced by first impressions. Just how well you present yourself depends on several factors ranging from the kind of car you drive, the clothes you wear, the self-confidence you generate, to what is telegraphed by your body language. For example, a receptionist (or prospect) may begin to size you up from the moment you're in view as you step out of your car. Obviously a freshly polished late-model luxury car creates a different impression than does a broken-down clunker. So does a well-groomed, smartly dressed salesperson versus a down-at-the-heels peddler wearing a frayed shirt and a weather-beaten sports jacket. The trimmings of success are vital. People form immediate impressions, based on first appearances, that either work for or against you.

How important is a winning image? Take, for example, the way in which one goes about selecting a surgeon. Obviously, it isn't possible to observe his work in surgery to predetermine his qualifications. Instead, we choose him by his projected image; we put our lives in his hands based on this perception. This same behavior dictates which attorneys we choose to represent us, which accountants prepare our income taxes, and which politicians operate our government. Similarly, people are far more likely to take the time to hear out a salesperson perceived to be successful and important than one who appears to be down and out.

In hardball selling, an image of success gets your foot in the door and sets the stage for your entire sales presentation. Without that image none of the concepts in this book will work. It's vital that you start off on the right foot. There are no second chances to make a strong first impression.

Getting Yourself Psyched Up

A hardball approach demands a hardball attitude. You must have conviction in your company, your product, and yourself. That conviction will be reflected in your body language, your facial expressions, and your tone of voice.

The best way I know to instill belief in yourself is by fully preparing yourself so that you *know* there is no curve a prospect can throw at you that will catch you off guard. To accomplish this, hardball salespeople do their homework— they know their business completely. They are professionals in every sense of the word—and everyone can see it. They have earned the respect they get from their customers.

What to Say to the Gatekeeper

Obviously, fitting the image of a hardball salesperson is only one part of the success formula that gets you past the gatekeeper. You must also have something to say to this person and, understandably, what you say is as essential as how you look.

Joe Gandolfo, who has sold more than a billion dollars of life insurance in a single year, thinks a salesperson's approach should generate an air of authority, "but I believe in giving as little information as possible to the gatekeeper." With a cold call, I simply say, 'Is Frank Brown in?' Often this is all it takes, so why go through a long explanation? The gatekeeper assumes that the boss knows me and I'm automatically led into his office."

Today, Gandolfo only makes cold calls by referrals, so when asked, "Does Mr. Brown know you?" he replies, "Dick Green suggested that I call Mr. Brown. Kindly tell him that I'm here to see him."

In the past, when his calls weren't always preceded by referrals, he would say, "I specialize in seeing people in the automobile industry, and I want to see Mr. Brown. Kindly tell him that I'm here to see him."

If asked what he is selling, Gandolfo assertively says, "I'm with Gandolfo Associates," and again he uses the line. "Kindly tell him that I want to see him."

"It is rare when a gatekeeper does not back off at this point," he explains, "but now and then, one says, 'I'm sorry but Mr. Brown isn't interested in talking to a salesman.'

" 'How do you know? Do you do his buying for him?' I fire back. Or I might say, 'He's not? This is the first time in thirty years I ever heard that. I've *got* to meet this man. I want to meet somebody who never talks to a salesman.' "

In the securities field, cold calls are made almost exclusively by telephone, but the principles are the same. Shearson Lehman Hutton's Martin Shafiroff, the nation's number one retail stockbroker, with annual commissions in excess of twelve million dollars, explains, "I always present myself pleasantly but in an authoritative manner. I speak firmly and never hesitate." Although he is America's top securities salesperson, he regularly makes six cold calls every day to maintain his sharpness. Many of these calls are made to CEOs and top executives of businesses ranging from privately owned multimillion-dollar corporations to the top Fortune 500 firms. His initial contact with the gatekeeper is direct and to the point: "I'd like to speak to Mr. Jeff Foster. Would you tell him Martin Shafiroff from New York is on the wire? I'm a managing director of Shearson Lehman Hutton."

"Most businesspeople know our firm, and I feel there is a psychological advantage in calling someone long-distance from one of Wall Street's most respected investment banking firms," Shafiroff explains. "It is true that a busy executive is more likely to get on the phone to speak with me than with a local stockbroker he has never met." There is no question that Shafiroff takes advantage of his position.

Richard Schultz, the founder and CEO of National Revenue Corporation, the nation's largest cash-flow management service firm, insists that a salesperson should never attempt to charm the gatekeeper because, "You'll come across like so many other salespersons who try to win her over, and she's on to them. She only becomes more suspicious that you're selling something and will go out of her way to give you a hard time."

Schultz insists that a salesperson loses control by volunteering too much information. "Give brief answers and question her," he suggests.

"Initially, I don't even give my name. I simply say, 'I'd like to talk to Mr. Williams.'

" 'Who shall I say is calling?'

" 'Richard Schultz. Is he in, please?'

" 'Yes. What company are you with?'

"At this point, I speak very slowly. 'National Revenue. Would you tell him I'm on the phone, please?'

"Notice that I've asked three times to be put through. I'm persistent, and I know I'll eventually win at what I refer to as a game of verbal volleyball. I anticipate her coming back with several screening questions. After all, that is her job and what she is paid to do. Sure, I could have easily said, 'This is Richard Schultz with National Revenue' on my first encounter with her, but I want her to ask for the information. Then, notice how I always answer her question with a question.

"Later, if she is persistent and asks the nature of my business, I say, 'It is a confidential financial matter. Would you please tell Mr. Williams that I would like to speak to him? If he is too busy, I will call back.'

"There are times when the prospect gets on the line and asks, 'Why didn't you mention you were calling about collecting delinquent accounts?' My stock answer is, 'National Revenue believes collecting delinquent accounts is a confidential matter, and customers usually appreciate any efforts we make not to announce our business to their employees.'"

IBM's Buck Rodgers, former vice president of worldwide marketing, uses a straightforward approach: "My name is Buck Rodgers, with IBM. I'd like to speak to Mr. Jones." It is admittedly easier to evoke initial interest with a prestigious company name like IBM, but it doesn't guarantee a shoo-in with every gatekeeper.

When Rodgers encounters some resistance, he says, "Look, I know you haven't met me, and I know your boss is a busy person. I also know that I have something really worthwhile to give him that will help him run his business, and he would want you to provide me with an opportunity to talk to him."

Now and then, Rodgers is told, "I'm sorry but he's unable to see you right now. Please give me your card and Mr. Jones will contact you if he's interested."

Here, Rodgers is more forceful and replies, "I know what your job entails from having my own secretary. I know it's difficult for you to decide whom Mr. Jones speaks to. I also realize that he's busy, but believe me, what I have to say is well worth his time. And I know he will appreciate that you gave me a chance to speak with him. Now would you please tell Mr. Jones that Buck Rodgers with IBM is here to see him?"

Have a Mission

On a cold call, you should always have a clearly defined mission, either to set up an appointment with the prospect or make an on-the-spot sales presentation. Once you set your objective, never deviate from it. The same advice applies whether you are making telephone or in-person calls.

For instance, an insurance agent might make a stop at a prospect's place of business to set up an appointment and be told: "As long as you're here, let's hear what you've got to sell."

While the temptation exists to give an on-the-spot presentation, I recommend that the agent stick to his initial game plan and say, "I'm sorry, but I only stopped in to introduce myself to you. I'm completely booked today, so let's set up a time to get together that's convenient for both of us." With this, he should take out his datebook and suggest the prospect do the same.

Two things are accomplished by doing this. First, the salesperson is presented as a successful person who has a busy schedule with limited time available. Second, salespeople who think they can come in unannounced and expect a prospect to drop everything to hear their sales presentation are sometimes viewed as having disrespect for other people's time. Therefore, in the above scenario, asking for an appointment rather than an immediate interview lets the insurance agent avoid insulting the prospect.

In some instances, a prospect will say: "You happened to catch me when I have the time available." After he looks through his date book, he adds: "It looks like I don't have an open date for weeks, so while you're here let's hear what you're selling."

Here you have two choices. First, going on the bird-in-the-hand theory, you can say: "Let me call my next appointment and see if I can reschedule it." (I advise saying this even if you don't have anything planned for the entire day.) Second, you can say: "I understand your position, however I only work by appointment, and I, too, am booked for several weeks in advance." Then after you look in your date book, you can continue: "I have nothing available during April. How does May 8th look for you?"

This technique makes you look as if your services are in great demand—the exact image you want to project. You also avoid giving a hurried presentation under less-than-ideal conditions. Mission accomplished.

Name-dropping

Dropping the right name opens a lot of otherwise closed doors. I, for one, am utterly amazed at how many doors have swung wide open for me by the mere mention of an influential person. If you have been referred to a prospect by a VIP, never keep it a secret.

The right names to use can fluctuate from a prospect's banker to his number one customer. Or it can be a person considered to be a community or social leader, a neighbor, a friend, brother-in-law, and so on. It works when, for whatever reason, the prospect does not want to risk offending a certain third party who sends you to see him.

For instance, Jerry Grant, a life insurance agent, calls on Harvey Borman, the president of a small chemical manufacturing company. Grant's Uncle Sam is a major customer of Borman's.

Grant introduces himself: "My name is Jerry Grant, with Fortune Life Insurance Company. I recently did some estate planning for my uncle, Sam Grant, and he suggested that you and I ought to get together. Uncle Sam speaks very highly of you, and he mentioned that you would show me the same courtesy that you would expect him to extend when you call on him. It's a pleasure to meet you, sir."

When Grant puts it this way, Borman is not going to risk offending a major customer's nephew by giving him the quick brush-off. By offending him, he may, in turn, offend Sam Grant.

Likewise, when Jean Kelly informs Larry Lancaster that she would like to meet with him to show him how Lancaster Printing can reduce its paper costs, Jean is going to be given an opportunity to present her wares. Why? Because her mother, Nellie Kelly, is chairperson of the nominating committee for the art museum's board of directors; Lancaster's wife, Bertha, desperately wants to join the board.

Having the right contacts plays a role in getting into places where you might not otherwise be permitted to enter, and it is appropriate to use them to serve as introductions on sales calls. I see no shame in having friends in high places and taking advantage of them to get your foot in the door. In fact, if you have such contacts and fail to capitalize on them, you are making your job unnecessarily difficult for yourself. Of course, it is one thing to have the right contacts and quite another to know how to use them. For instance, Jean Kelly had to find out in advance that Larry Lancaster's wife, Bertha, wanted so badly to be on the art museum's board. Again, you must do your homework so your contacts can serve to your advantage.

If you happen to know a top-ranking executive of a large corporation, say the CEO, president, or an executive vice president, often he or she may refer you to a lower-ranked person in charge of buying your product. For example, Louis Stevenson might ask his golfing buddy, Sid Greenstreet, the CEO of First Bank, for the name of the person at the bank who has the authority to purchase advertising specialties. Then, upon introducing himself, Stevenson says: "I'm with Ace Products, and Sid Greenstreet said that you were the person for me to contact at the bank...."

Get Down to Business

Once past the gatekeeper and into the prospect's office, the same hardball selling principles are applicable. Here, too, you must project an air of importance and professionalism. Again, you must speak authoritatively. If you come across as a stereotypical salesperson, you are going to reduce your chances of making your sales presentation. While the prospect may value the gatekeeper's judgment, remember he is the boss and ultimately decides with whom he will talk.

Too often salespeople think small talk is the way to soften a prospect before the presentation. I disagree. This is not the time to flatter him about the mounted sailfish above his mantel or listen to him discuss his golf game, his tropical fish collection, or the World Series. Nor is it appropriate to tell a joke or to talk politics or any other non-business-related subject. In fact, if the prospect does any of these things, I have often said: "If it's okay with you, I suggest that we get right down to business, and later, if time permits, I'd be delighted to hear more about that." While on the surface this may seem somewhat unfriendly, it always works.

"But isn't a salesperson supposed to talk about what interests the customer?" I am asked. This is exactly how ordinary salespeople think. A hardball salesperson avoids this trap. His objective is to project a higher level of professionalism, and he places his or her time at a premium. When a prospect realizes that you are, indeed, different, he or she will react differently. For this reason, I advocate a strict no-nonsense-get-right-down-to-business approach.

Furthermore, looking at things from the prospect's viewpoint, successful people don't have time to discuss nonbusiness matters during their workday. They often resent salespeople who waste their valuable time on trivial matters. It angers me when a salesperson calls me during the day and says: "Hello, Mr. Shook. How are you today?"

"I'm fine," I respond.

"Are you enjoying this beautiful day?"

"I haven't had an opportunity to get outside today," I reply abruptly.

"Say, I love your office building."

"Look," I finally say, "What's on your mind? Or did you just call to make small talk?"

I view such interruptions as an intrusion. I especially feel this way when a telephone solicitor calls and starts off the conversation as if he or she is somebody I am supposed to know. "Hello, Bob. This is Joan Rollins. How are you today?"

"Er, fine," I mutter, trying to place the name.

"It certainly is a beautiful day, isn't it?"

She was doing fine until this remark. Now, I suspect she's a telephone solicitor making a cold call. "Yeah," I reply. "I'm very busy right now."

"If this is a bad time, I'll call you back . . ."

"What are you selling?" I ask abruptly.

I don't like to give a salesperson, of all people, a rough time. After all, I've had my share of cold calls and I know what he or she has to do to make a living. But I do get upset when a salesperson calls and uses an unprofessional approach. Professionalism is all I ask, and then I'm easy.

Do you see what happens? The prospect takes a combative position and the salesperson starts out being on the defensive. The friendly approach results in an unfriendly relationship, putting two strikes against the salesperson before he has a chance to get his bat off his shoulder.

Resourcefulness

When I was twenty-three, during my first year as an insurance agent, I was given the name of a farmer whom I considered a hot lead. I drove thirty miles out of my way to see him, and upon arriving at the farm, I spotted him working on his tractor in the

49

middle of a large field of wheat. It was a blistering summer day, which I interpreted as a good reason for a farmer to take a break from the hot sun. I parked my car at the side of the country road and walked about a hundred yards in his direction. When I came into view, he drove across the field to me, turned off his engine, and yelled: "This better be important."

As he climbed off his tractor and approached me, the ground seemed to shake. He was six feet five inches and easily weighed 250 pounds. He looked like the biggest, meanest man I had ever seen.

When I identified myself I could see his blood pressure elevate. "I swore I'd take the next son of a bitch who tried to sell me insurance," he shouted, "and throw him bodily off my land."

I looked him straight in the eye and said: "Let me tell you something, my friend. Before you try anything like that with me, you better take out all the insurance you can get because you're going to need it."

There was a moment of silence and I didn't bat an eyelash. Neither did he. Then he burst out laughing. "What the hell, on a hot day like this, I could use a break. Come on over to the house and let's hear what you've got." He put his arm around my shoulder and we headed toward his house.

We walked into his kitchen, and he said to his wife: "Hey, honey, I want you to meet Bob Shook. Do you want to hear a good one? This little guy thinks he could take me." We all enjoyed a laugh at my expense, but when we got down to business, it turned out to be one of the easiest sales I had ever made.

Now you might think: "I'm not that quick-witted. Besides, I would never have the nerve to say that." But if I did it, you can do it too. First, I was not as quick-witted as it appears on the surface. Earlier in my career, when somebody threatened to throw me out, I did back down and retreated like a whipped dog. I didn't like the feeling and I vowed that, in the future, I would always hold my head high when I walked out. Actually, it was several weeks before my encounter with the farmer that I came up with my line. So much for my quick-wittedness. What's more, I was not nearly as bold as it may seem. What I lacked in quickness of wit, I made up with in quickness of foot. I knew that if the huge farmer really meant to take a swing at me, I could always outrun him. I never felt actually threatened by any real danger of physical harm.

Much of the credit for the success I enjoy as an author goes to the seventeen years I spent in sales prior to beginning my writing career. I have been able to apply to my present profession many of the selling techniques I learned as a salesperson, and this has helped me immensely. In 1980, when I authored *The Real Estate People,* I profiled ten of the industry's most successful individuals, including Harry Helmsley, whose net worth of nearly two billion dollars makes him one of America's richest people. My first task was to set up a three-hour interview with Helmsley, and, believe me, it was no simple task to even get to talk to his private secretary. When I did, it was only to be told: "If you call Mr. Helmsley on Friday morning at 10:08, I will put you down for a five-minute telephone conversation with him."

At exactly 10:07, I placed the call. I was disappointed to have his secretary inform me: "I'm sorry, but an emergency came up and Mr. Helmsley is out of the office for the day." Another appointment for a five-minute telephone conversation with Helmsley was rescheduled for the following Thursday at 2:44 P.M.

Again, I called at 2:44 and was once more told: "Mr. Helmsley is tied up but you can call him on Monday at 11:27 A.M."

Finally, on my third call, I was put through. Knowing I had only a few minutes in which to set up an appointment, I gave him a quick explanation about the book I was writing and told him I wanted to write a chapter about him.

"Mr. Shook," he began, "give me one reason why I should be in your book. What will it specifically do for me?"

"Mr. Helmsley, I can't think of how being in my book can personally benefit you," I replied. "But there is one very good reason why you should consider an interview with me."

"What's that?" he asked.

"The real estate business has been very good to you, Mr. Helmsley."

"Yes," he interrupted, "it's been very, very good to me."

"As a way of paying back your dues," I continued, "I believe that you should share your philosophy and knowledge with others. Doing so will upgrade the real estate profession, and you will be performing a good deed for America."

There was a brief pause, and he said: "Would you kindly send me a letter giving a brief explanation of your book? And then call me in a couple of weeks."

"I'll be delighted to do so, Mr. Helmsley."

That afternoon, I sent him an overnight package that included a two-page cover letter, my bio sketch, three Shook books, and some newspaper and magazine articles about my writing career.

The following afternoon, my secretary came into my office and announced: "You have a phone call from Harry."

I picked up the receiver and the person said: "Mr. Shook, this is Harry."

"Harry who?" I questioned.

"This is Harry Helmsley, and I reviewed your material. I'd be honored to be in your book, Mr. Shook."

"That's great, Harry," I blurted out. I thought to myself: "That's a good one. I'm calling him Harry, and he's calling me Mr. Shook."

"What's a good time for me to see you, sir? I'll come to New York at your convenience," I said.

"You name the time, and I'll make sure I'm available," Helmsley told me.

"How's next Tuesday morning at 10:37 sharp?" I asked.

Fortunately, Helmsley recognized my intended humor and laughed. "I'll see you at 10:37 on Tuesday morning," he confirmed.

I was equipped to answer Helmsley's initial question because it was one that I had been asked by other highly successful people. I had been turned down by two other leading businesspersons I attempted to interview, so I had prepared myself for him when he asked, "What's in it for me?" I did, however, ad-lib the 10:37 A.M. comment, which, while humorous, was not a deciding factor in getting the interview. As you can see, resourcefulness is not synonymous with spontaneity. While it would be nice, you don't have to possess the wit of a Johnny Carson or a Robin Williams to give quick and sharp rebuttals while being interrogated by a prospect. In fact, as the salesperson, you have the upper hand because you can draw upon past experiences to come prepared for anticipated curves that might be thrown at you. The prospect does not have this advantage.

I also want to point out something I was fortunate enough to learn early in my sales career. People are people, both small and big. Hardball selling tactics are equally effective with *everyone*—ranging from a farmer who farms 160 acres in western Pennsylvania to a real estate baron who owns more than five hundred high-rise buildings in New York City, including the Empire State Building!

A Touch of Thick Skin

Hardball selling necessitates having thick skin. It is not meant for the meek whose feelings are easily bruised.

Yet a hardball salesperson will only encounter a fraction of the rejection directed at the conventional seller because he or she is not the type of individual to be intimidated. Now and then, however, there is the danger that a strong approach will alienate a prospect. When this happens, there is the likelihood that a harsh chewing out may ensue.

I am willing to accept this as an inherent risk that comes with the territory. As a percentage player, I am willing to endure an occasional small dose of rejection to realize sufficient long-term gains. In retrospect, I confess to having been shaken up earlier in my career when a prospect came down hard on me for using a hardball approach. I am no different from anyone else—I never liked rejection and I never will. Nor have I ever met a salesperson who felt differently. It is understandable to dislike rejection; however, it is unacceptable to be discouraged and defeated by it.

You must be tough and tenacious. When you are, an interesting phenomenon will occur—you will rarely encounter hostility. Because the more adept and confident you are with your approach, the better reception you will receive.

The Lean and Mean Look

I believe physical fitness must be a top priority for every salesperson. No matter how well dressed an individual is, obesity or emaciation ruins an otherwise good appearance. Even the finest clothing has its limitations when covering a neglected body.

A salesperson in excellent physical condition projects a good first impression for several reasons. First and foremost, it indicates high self-esteem because taking good care of oneself requires effort. A person who abuses his body is likely to have a poor opinion of himself. Second, being in top shape necessitates discipline; for most of us it is no easy task to maintain a good physique. Third, physical fitness provides stamina and extra energy. All of these are admirable qualities that generate positive images. For this reason many sales organizations seek former college and professional athletes.

To paint a vivid picture of how the lean and mean look works, wouldn't it be much more difficult to resist a six-four ex-NFL linebacker who came charging into your office than a grossly overweight marshmallow-type salesman who has to catch his breath between sentences? If you're not into sports analogies, visualize how you would react to a salesperson who was an ex-Marine drill sergeant—his walk has a certain swagger conveying self-assuredness, mental toughness, and authority. This is not the type of person you would want to cross.

As an extra and important bonus, being in top physical shape reduces fatigue and increases mental sharpness; each can be a deciding factor in closing a difficult sale at the end of a long day. The hardball salesperson is hard, and prospects know it.

3

How to Win Sales, Not Friends

During the past five decades, Dale Carnegie's classic book, *How to Win Friends and Influence People*, has enjoyed immense popularity, especially among salespeople. However, I have one problem with the book. Its title should read the other way around: How to Influence People and Win Friends.

Too many salespeople share the erroneous opinion that prospects must be converted into friends *before* the sale is closed. For the record, I neither oppose selling to friends nor befriending buyers. In fact, I believe that not selling to one's friends is doing them an injustice. Likewise, I have no objections to socializing with customers, but there is a time and place for everything. The number one priority during a sales presentation is to influence a person to buy, not to make a friend.

Rid yourself of the notion that a customer has to like you before he will place an order. Fulfilling his needs and winning his respect are what really count. Do these things and you will eventually win his friendship; it will be the by-product. Don't sell yourself as the primary product. You are not in business to make friends.

Don't get me wrong. I'm not suggesting being aloof; this is not the place to be *unfriendly*. But you must avoid being like those salespeople who lay it on so thick that they appear superficial. They are overeager and too obliging; while they may have good intentions, they scare away more prospects than they attract.

It is important to keep in mind that because salespeople are driven by monetary gain, the relationship between a salesperson and customer is vastly different from one between friends. Because the seller's remuneration is predicated on closing the sale, solicitation predicated on friendly overtures smacks of insincerity, hardly the cornerstone upon which a permanent relationship is built.

Please, No Flattery

Attempting to win over customers with hollow compliments has been around since the invention of the commission. Certainly, every salesperson has been guilty of making flattering remarks that were spoken with the sole intent of influencing a sale. For the most part, it is done innocently, on the pretext that inducing prospects to like us will influence them to buy our products.

It is natural to say nice things in hopes of receiving favors. We begin to do so as children and continue to do so throughout our lives. It is tempting to believe that big orders can result from massaging the big egos of successful people. However, you are only deceiving yourself by thinking flattery will produce additional sales. Today's buying public is too smart for such cheap shots. By stroking customers' egos, you cast yourself in the same role as the countless salespeople who have preceded you. Buyers are offended by blatant attempts to get their business with false praise and are fed up with the backslappers who will say anything to make a sale. Flattery doesn't just fail to butter up prospects; it often undermines otherwise effective sales presentations.

You must eliminate all traces of flattery from your repertoire. It has no place in the sales profession and is counterproductive to successful hardball selling.

Gifts of Obligation

How many times have you walked into an automobile agency to have the salesman hand you a small gift such as a coffee mug or calendar? How often has an insurance agent, upon introducing himself, presented you with a ballpoint pen or a pocket-size datebook? I know of at least three different direct-mail companies in the office supplies field that offer enticements to their customers, ranging from pocket calculators to color television sets.

There are salespeople who offer Super Bowl tickets to customers; there are the Las Vegas gambling casinos that compliment ("comp") their big-spending customers with first-class airfare, plush suites, and front-row nightclub seats.

In each of these incidents, the customer is given a gift of obligation with the intent to make the buyer feel obligated to do business with the seller. Smart buyers understand, however, that there is no such thing as a free lunch. Nobody gives away something for nothing. There are always strings attached. They know that the cost of hotel suites, tickets, and color television sets is built into the price of the product, which is ultimately passed on to the customer. Buyers realize that the free television set has a value of, say, three hundred dollars. And most buyers, if given a choice, would prefer to have this cost deducted from the order. American consumers are not naive; they are aware of these transparent tactics. Even when the gift is one they might have purchased on its own merit, it causes unnecessary suspicion and resentment that works against the sales effort.

The time has come to stop the use of giveaways and recognize it as merely a gimmick. Even teachers do not receive polished apples anymore because today's students are smart enough to know it doesn't score points, it causes suspicion. Yet, there are many salespeople out there who seem to have missed that lesson, and keep polishing those unwanted apples.

A gift of obligation is also a sales deterrent because it is unrelated to the actual sales transaction. Offers of payola insult the buyer's integrity as well as compromising the salesperson's. In my estimation, a salesperson prostitutes himself by offering any type of favor for a business transaction. But more important, attaching a gimmick to your product implies that it cannot compete on its own in the marketplace. I don't think there is any place for this kind of selling today. Although, on the surface, small gifts are considered legitimate business expenses, this practice is paramount to slipping a few bucks under the table to get the buyer's business. Sell on the merit of your product; it isn't necessary to give anything away to make a sale.

Fear of Rejection

For the most part, salespeople are extroverted because introverts are simply not attracted to our line of work. As extroverts, we want people to like us and we crave acceptance. With this in mind, it should come as no surprise that most of us have difficulty dealing with rejection.

Let's analyze what happens. During the course of a presentation, an outgoing, likeable salesperson builds up a rapport with a prospect. Until it is time to close the sale there is generally only marginal resistance. Toward the end of the sales interview, the communication between seller and buyer reaches a peak and a camaraderie evolves. The moment of truth comes when the request for the order is made. Now it is time for the prospect to make a buying decision. This is the most critical moment in the sales presentation.

From prior experience, most salespersons anticipate that a reluctance to buy will occur, and any effort exerted to motivate the prospect to make a buying decision brings with it the risk that he will be antagonized. What was perceived as the beginning of a beautiful friendship can come to an abrupt end. To avoid the unpleasantness of possible rejection while attempting to close the sale, the typical salesperson draws in his reins and backs off. He takes the cowardly way out and continues to talk, conveniently circumventing the risk of rejection. Ironically, trying to avoid a "no" makes the odds of getting that "no" increase dramatically.

To compound the problem, nobody likes to be obviously high-pressured into making a buying decision. And every salesperson understands that if he appears to use high-pressure tactics, he may indeed offend the buyer. Yet, without exerting high pressure, it is probable that a sale that is makable will dissipate. Here is where a typical salesperson faces what he considers a real dilemma, and he asks himself the question: "Should I risk pushing the prospect and thereby offend him? Or should I ease off?" Admittedly, it is difficult for most salespeople to take an aggressive position and go for the close. Their tendency is to back off and avoid confrontation. Just how one reacts at this critical crossroads is bound to have a considerable bearing on one's sales career.

A more aggressive response that focuses on never giving in to a callback might cause some initial friction, but it is the percentage play advocated throughout the entirety of this book. When you elect to sell hardball you have accepted the fact that some prospects will resist your high-pressure efforts to close the sale. Some will let you know their displeasure, and they will do so in no uncertain terms. They will be very vocal, and on occasion, strongly express their annoyance. Just the same, hang in there—by doing so, you will ultimately get more than your share of sales. To me, the added commissions are worth the discomfort that the occasional rejection causes.

Don't expect the prospect to come to your aid. It is easier for him to delay buying decisions, and he will do his best to lure you into trivial conversation or some other diversion intended to sidetrack you. Although there is much temptation to give in to yet another diversion, stay on track. Continue your presentation and close. You must be strong-willed and single-purposed. If you allow yourself to be sidetracked, you will be derailed.

For example, during an insurance agent's close of an annuity policy to fund a college education, a prospect goes off on a tangent about raising children in today's complicated society. "They have it too easy today," he complains. "We're spoiling them."

Rather than agreeing, the agent directs the conversation back to the merits of his product. "This policy is currently paying a truly incredible rate of interest: nine percent. In the event of your death, the premium is paid, thereby guaranteeing your daughter's education. Isn't it comforting to know that you will never have to worry about her future, Stanley?"

In the above example, the agent wisely refused to get drawn into an irrelevant conversation about the problems with young people. A typical salesperson's inclination is to agree with the prospect and reply with a comment such as: "Yeah, in my day, I worked two part-time jobs to pay my way through school. My kids think going to Florida for spring break is a necessity." Not only does a remark of this nature have nothing to do with the need for a life insurance annuity, but it opens the door for the prospect to continue the discussion, thereby further distracting the buyer and seller and creating an even greater chance of losing the sale by default.

Throughout this book, I will remind you: *When it is time to close the sale, close the sale.* Sadly, salespeople often don't know when to stop. They tend to oversell and fail to close sales that should have been made. "It makes no sense," you may say, "for anyone to talk too much and thereby jeopardize a sale." It may make sense, because a salesperson fears rejection, but it makes no sale. High pressure makes sales.

So often there is a tendency to skirt the main issue in what is almost certain to be a vain attempt to maintain rapport with the prospect. You must rid yourself of the thought that it is necessary to gain a prospect's acceptance by talking about subjects he chooses to discuss. I do not dispute that a fear of rejection prevails, but you must never submit to it. Rejection will occur sometimes. Accept it as coming with the territory. The good news is that when you master hardball selling, you'll encounter less rejection.

Don't Shortchange a Friend

There is a tendency for salespeople to give watered-down sales presentations to endearing acquaintances such as friends and relatives. They underestimate the effort required to make these "easy" sales and think a less-than-full explanation is sufficient to do the job. Their friends get shortchanged because not enough facts were provided to make a buying decision. As a result of not being properly sold, they are not "sure sales" after all.

No matter how much interest a friend or relative expresses, you must not allow your closeness with them to interfere with what should be treated as a business relationship. For instance, while you may be tempted to sell somebody at a dinner party, on the golf course, or at a backyard cookout, you must explain: "This isn't the time or place to discuss business, and besides, that's not why I'm here today." Then set up an appointment in an environment that works in your favor—without distractions. Furthermore, be careful not to give away bits of information in informal settings where you may be told: "I have enough information, and if I'm interested, I'll call you." More often than not, mixing business with pleasure backfires. Social contacts are wonderful for getting your foot in the door, but I recommend avoiding on-the-spot sales presentations. Use these contacts to set up future appointments where the atmosphere will be conducive to conducting business.

Never take anyone for granted. Nobody should be viewed as an automatic sale. Every prospect, even your best friend or brother, deserves to hear a complete sales presentation. Treat them with the same respect and courtesy you extend to all of your clients. It is unfair to penalize friends because of your relationship with them. Then, too, there is a tendency to apply less high pressure on relatives and friends. This is natural, but you aren't doing them a favor by making it easy for them to procrastinate. Over the years, I have heard many salespeople complain that their friends and relatives buy "much less than you would expect" from them. With a watered-down sales presentation and a no-pressure close, what else could they expect?

No More Mr. Nice Guy

I have never been sure what Leo Durocher had in mind when he said, "Nice guys finish last," because it is difficult for me to understand how being nice is detrimental to baseball players. But Durocher did deliver a solid message to salespeople. In selling, the Mr. Nice Guy approach is self-destructive.

For the record, I see nothing wrong with being nice to people; treating them with courtesy and respect is a must. However, a sales presentation should be conducted as strictly business, and a salesperson should not turn it into a popularity contest. As a salesperson, you are supposed to care about your prospect's business and your own business. You are not supposed to say whatever customers want to hear in order to get their business. By doing so, you become a "yes man," and yes men are annoying and generally discounted.

Rid yourself of happy-face pins, particularly those that read: Have a Nice Day! Throw away those bumper stickers informing other drivers that you brake for small animals. You can still brake them—just don't advertise it. This is not the business image that a hardball salesperson needs to project.

It is inappropriate to be overly thankful to a prospect for being granted an interview to give a sales presentation. I get chills down my spine when I hear a salesman say: "I realize that you are a very busy man, Mr. Finkelman, and I want you to know how thankful I am that you would give me a few minutes of your valuable time." While to some, this appears to be a polite way to begin a presentation, I think it reduces a salesman to the ranks of a second-class citizen. A hardball salesperson views himself as an equal to the prospect. His time is equally valuable. This kind of sweet talk suggests that the prospect is doing you a favor by hearing you out. It elevates the prospect to a higher position, and as a result, places him in control of the sale.

The real danger in being Mr. Nice Guy is that nobody minds saying no to him. Mr. Milquetoast doesn't put up any resistance, so people don't mind rejecting him. After all, he won't make a whimper—he'll just take it on the chin, smile, and go on to his next call. The salesperson to whom it is difficult to say no is the one who won't let anyone off the hook without applying some forceful persuasion. I can assure you that by the time someone has given me a final no, he will have had to justify his decision from every conceivable direction.

Being Firm and Forthright

Several years ago, I ghostwrote a best-selling autobiography of one of the nation's most dynamic and best-known women. While I am not at liberty to give you her name, be assured that she is one of America's most successful self-made businesswomen.

I visited her offices to sell myself as her ghostwriter, and at the point in our discussion when she asked me my fee, I replied: "There are many authors who are willing to write for a relatively small fee. But that's not my style. I work on a fifty-fifty split of all royalties generated. Whatever you get, I get the same. If the book is a big seller, I'll get paid what I'm worth. And if it isn't, I will also get paid what I'm worth."

At the time, the going rate for ghostwriting a book of this nature was approximately twenty-five thousand dollars; I was asking for an equal split of all earnings from the book, including video and audio. The woman was obviously savvy about the flat fees commonly paid to writers, and such an arrangement would have provided her with the lion's share of the royalties. She listened carefully to me, then said: "Aren't you asking for a lot of money, Mr. Shook?"

"Yes ma'am," I replied. "In fact, on this basis, if the book does as well as I anticipate, we will have a major best-seller and I'll be the most expensive ghostwriter in America." I paused and repeated, "Yes, I have no doubt that it will make me the most expensive ghostwriter in the country."

"That's fine with me," she said approvingly, "because I always like to work with the best."

I closed the sale because I was firm and forthright with her.

I didn't beat around the bush, telling her what she wanted to hear. What I did do was speak with confidence, which signaled to her that I was good at my work. Furthermore, I made no attempt to negotiate how much I should be paid. In similar circumstances, I have heard salespeople offer lame reasons to justify high fees. For example: "I have a lot of personal expenses, three children to educate, and my wife just lost her job. I need more than twenty-five thousand dollars in order to meet my current cost of living." While it might be true that you need more than the going rate, there is no reason why a buyer should be willing to pay a higher figure. If you can't afford to live within your means, that is your problem, not the customer's.

When salespeople hesitate to say anything they think the prospect might find objectionable, they weaken their position. Be direct and to the point. You cannot operate from a position of strength by hiding that strength.

Illusions

All too often salespeople walk out of a prospect's office full of enthusiasm and in high spirits—without having made a sale! This amazes me. While it is wrong to go into a state of depression, neither should salesmen become euphoric without having received an order.

During my years as a sales manager in the insurance field, it was not unusual for my agents to call me at my home in the evenings to report how their day went.

"I had a great day," a salesman would declare.

"Terrific. Tell me about it," I'd say, expecting to hear about new clients signed.

"Well, I didn't actually close a sale, but I had two calls and really hit it off with both of them..."

"Wait a minute. If you didn't make a sale today," I'd interrupt, "then you didn't have a great day. In fact, you had a bad day."

Too often, salespeople are under the impression that a sales presentation went well because they were the recipient of friendly treatment by a prospect. They are misinterpreting a warm reception as sales production, when, in fact, it is not. Pats on the back, warm greetings, goodbye hugs, and other friendly gestures are not measurements of success in the sales field and should not be considered as such. Nor are interests expressed in your product, compliments about your sales presentation, or requests to leave brochures.

It has been said that every time a sales presentation is made and the salesperson leaves on a cheerful note, a sale is made. This statement implies that the prospect, not you, makes a sale even though you left his office with a blank order pad. Sometimes prospects may be charming, and they can make you feel as good as if you have just walked out with a large order. But the facts are, no sale is no sale. Hardball salespeople are bottom-line-oriented. Nothing other than a closed sale is acceptable.

4

Having an Edge

The doctrine of democracy extols the virtue of equality but equality is not relevant in the world of selling. A hardball salesperson strives to obtain a disproportionately large piece of the pie; his quest for an edge over the competition never ceases. In every sales situation each salesperson possesses certain qualities unlike those of the competition. It is not always possible to compare apples with apples; many variables exist that make comparisons difficult. While one salesperson scores high marks in one area, another beats him somewhere else. A hardball salesperson is continually striving to maximize his competitive edge; the attainment of success rests on attaining this advantage.

When You Got It, Flaunt It

Selling is a profession in which one can ill afford false modesty. Every advantage you possess should be promoted at every opportunity.

To sell hardball, you can't be bashful about telling others about the extraordinary qualities of your merchandise, the high-principled company you represent, or that you are service-driven and excel in your field. If you sell the best, never hesitate to tell it to others. And even if your product doesn't knock the socks off the competition in every aspect, emphasize those advantages that illustrate your superiority. Remember there are few products that ever dominate an industry across the board, so sell whatever quality you have that the competition doesn't have.

A thin line exists between a superseller and a blowhard. While you don't want to omit a strong sales point where you have an important edge over the competition, neither do you want to come across as a boaster. An automobile salesperson, for example, might explain: "Many of our customers tell us how courteous and thoughtful our service department people are. Customers rave about how our firm does backbends to satisfy their needs." By putting it this way, the salesman doesn't sound as if he is making an idle boast; instead, he sounds humble and sincere. This subtle technique is more effective than saying: "We have the best service department in town." Likewise, an insurance agent might say: "Our net cost is rated the best value in the life insurance industry." This is more gentle than to brag: "No other insurer comes close to our net cost." Nor should a real estate broker boast: "I have the best listings of homes in town." Instead, the broker should say: "I have a wide selection of homes in your price range; and, in fact, some other brokers say I have the best selection of homes in town." As you can see, there is a subtle way to flavor what you offer that tells the same message but, at the same time, doesn't come across as too strong and put people on guard.

Turning a Disadvantage into an Advantage

Practically every disadvantage can be converted into an advantage. A classic example is when Avis did its We're-number-two-so-we-try-harder campaign. The company promoted its second-place position as an advantage over Hertz, the number one firm in the car rental business. To my knowledge, nobody had ever previously presented its number two position as an advantage over its leading competition. But it worked.

Often described as the most powerful personal manager in show business, Jay Bernstein is a man who well understands how to turn disadvantages into advantages. Bernstein is the Hollywood agent who discovered Farrah Fawcett, Suzanne Somers, and Linda Evans; he has represented more than six hundred stars including Susan Hayward, William Holden, Burt Lancaster, Sammy Davis, Jr., and Frank Sinatra. Yet early in his career, when Bernstein operated a tiny office out of his girlfriend's apartment, his refrigerator and stove were used as his filing cabinets, and an old ironing board held his typewriter.

His first major client, actor Joel Grey, had been referred to Bernstein by a mutual friend. Grey needed a lot of convincing to drop his established firm, a nationally known PR company. The fledging agent had his work cut out for him.

"Sure, I'm a new PR firm," Bernstein explained, "so I've got to prove myself by the work I do for you. You can go with somebody else and pay two and three times as much, but you won't get two and three times the work." Bernstein even used his hole-in-the-wall offices as a selling point. "The big firms have a tremendous overhead, and their clients are the ones who ultimately pay for it. What's more, they assign some new kid in the business to handle your account. With me, you're dealing with senior management. At the fees I charge, I'm the best bargain in town."

Bernstein turned every disadvantage into a selling point. "I'm hungry and aggressive, so you're going to get a lot more for a lot less with me as your agent. I'm on call twenty-four hours a day, seven days a week. Whenever you need me, I'm as near as your telephone. I promise you that you'll never find anyone else who will work as hard for you."

Bernstein realized that being unmarried could work against him. Many prospects preferred an older married man who would be more settled and therefore perceived as more reliable. Some also thought that a married man had more responsibilities so he would be more motivated. Being a bachelor on the Hollywood scene carried with it a playboy image, hardly one to promote reliability and stability. Again, Bernstein used his single status to his advantage; "I don't have a wife and kids to rush home to, and I don't have a family to take skiing over the weekend." It's no wonder Jay Bernstein is immensely successful. He sees every circumstance as an advantage.

When my own company was in its beginning stages, I told prospects: "We're a budding company, but I promise you that we will someday be the leader in our industry. You have an opportunity to join us while we are still on the ground floor. And because we are small, we're light on our feet and we'll do things for you that the giant bureaucratic companies can't do. Besides, you are a very important client to us. With the big companies, your business will be viewed as insignificant and you'll be given little attention." The emphasis was placed on why it was an advantage to be small.

Later, when we became a larger company, my rationale changed: "We're the leader in our industry. And there is a reason why we are. We became big because we give the best value, the best service, and we care about each customer. We deserve to be the leader in our field because we've earned it with superior service. And we have no intention of ever relinquishing our top position. As a large company, we have the resources and the backup people to serve you in a way that a small company simply cannot. And even though we are a big company, we take pride in being light on our feet; we still operate with a small-company mentality. We are number one and we will stay on top because we are very good at what we do."

It's a simple formula. When we were small, we promoted smallness as an advantage. We had the ability to give personal attention and maintain lightness of foot. When we were big, we demonstrated why it was advantageous to do business with a big company; we had an enormous wealth of resources and backup service people. If you think it through, most disadvantages can be presented as advantages. Be creative.

Never Knock the Competition . . . and Be Obvious About it!

It is an exhibition of poor taste to knock the competition. The old adage, "If you don't have something good to say about somebody, don't say anything," is still good advice. People would rather be sold on the benefits of your product than on a competitor's shortcomings.

Magazine and television commercials that knock other companies are, in effect, promoting their competition. For instance, when a computer company makes comparisons about how its product stacks up against IBM, IBM receives free advertising. Furthermore, most people are fed up with companies that sell their products based on stated weaknesses of a competitor. This may occasionally work in politics, but it is inappropriate in business. Sometimes a buyer, as does a voter, interprets this kind of selling to be unsportsmanlike and underhanded.

Now that I've said that knocking the competition can be detrimental, let me tell you how to do it so subtly you can shed a poor light on the other guy without making yourself look bad. The most effective way I know to knock a competitor is to deliver your message through somebody else. For instance, a copier salesperson might say: "Dave White, the office manager at the law firm of Katz, Wolfe, Fox and Baehr told me, 'It takes about three days to get ABC Copiers to respond to a service call.' I can't believe that kind of down time. Fortunately, our company has a reputation for immediate service." So here, a third person, in this case an office manager, is knocking the competition, not the salesperson.

Super car salesman Joe Girard used to collect negative articles on all automobile manufacturers. If a prospect mentioned wanting to shop around to look at, say, a Chrysler, Joe would take out several news clippings ranging from poor performance to low safety ratings on Chryslers. It didn't matter what car a prospect wanted to compare to Girard's Chevrolets; whatever the interest was, Girard had in hard print why it shouldn't be a consideration. "The negative information was conveyed, but I never personally knocked the competition," he explains.

How many times have you witnessed an auto salesman maliciously attack a competitor? For instance, he might say: "You want to shop around and look at Jaguars? What are you, a masochist? You must enjoy having your car rust out. Well, if you buy a Jag, I recommend buying a second one because the first one will always be in the garage." This kind of antagonistic attack insults the customer's intelligence. The salesman, by ridiculing his judgment, is bound to cause resentment, hostility, and a defensive stance. You can get the same message across with the application of subtlety—let somebody else make the same point. A top life insurance agent I know asks his new clients to write a letter to him stating why they dropped XYZ Company's policy and replaced it with his. By getting local people in the community to state their dissatisfaction, they do his criticizing without him having to utter a word.

Showing letters and new articles instead of verbally assaulting the competition has another advantage: *The printed word carries more weight than the spoken word.* A negative statement in print conveys more credibility than one stated verbally by a salesman. This is true because as a salesperson you are suspected of having the ulterior motive of making the competition look bad. However, the letter writer is a once-removed disinterested party. Plus there is the fact that many people still believe "if it is written, it is true."

A favorite way of mine to knock the opposition is by not acknowledging it as a competitor. The less said, the better. For instance, a prospect who was considering doing business with another company once asked me what I thought about them. "I don't think about them," I simply replied and continued with my sales presentation. It worked like a charm.

Packaging Yourself

While not everyone can have the looks and style of a Gary Cooper, a lot can be done to make the most of one's appearance and, likewise, project an image of success. Perhaps a place to start, and one involving relatively little expense, is to upgrade your wardrobe. Dressing like a successful sales executive helps create a favorable first impression—winners like to do business with winners. If an extensive wardrobe is not affordable, I recommend quality rather than quantity. It's better to have two fine suits than a dozen cheap ones. (You actually only need to own a single suit to make a good first impression, but on occasion, it requires a quick visit to the cleaners.)

When my twenty-three-year-old son RJ began his career as a stockbroker with Prudential Bache Securities in Hilton Head, South Carolina, I served as his "wardrobe consultant" by taking him on a shopping spree to buy several dark pin-striped suits and the necessary accoutrements. "But the other securities salesmen don't wear dark suits, Dad. They wear sport jackets and some only wear dress shirts with a tie. It's a very casual atmosphere on the island," he told me.

"Trust me on this one," I advised him. "Besides, it's on me."

We picked out four expensive suits, a half-dozen button-down dress shirts, some conservative British-type ties, black wingtip shoes, and yes, two pairs of suspenders.

Late in the afternoon of his first day on the job, RJ called and sounded somewhat down. "Thanks to you, Dad, everyone's calling me 'Mr. Wall Street.'"

"Perfect," I replied. "If you're going to be a stockbroker, isn't this exactly the image you want to project? Imagine you're a retired person who just relocated to Hilton Head and you want to check out the local Prudential Bache office for a broker to handle your account. If you see eight guys sitting at their desks dressed casually and another dressed as if he just stepped out of the movie *Wall Street*, which would get your attention? Don't be concerned about having people nickname you 'Mr. Wall Street.' That's not a bad way to be identified in your business."

RJ agreed that my advice was sound, and he continues to dress conservatively. Even during those hot South Carolina summer days, he doesn't deviate from projecting his investment banker image. He is successful and I am sure that his appearance gives him an edge over many of the local Hilton Head stockbrokers. Other stockbrokers have rationalized that their appearance plays only a minor role in their business because the vast majority of their time is devoted to telephone selling and little contact is made with the general public. I think they fail to realize the importance of their occasional face-to-face meetings with clients, and, in particular, their initial contacts to generate new business. Then too, a salesperson's self-concept is detectable over the telephone. Feeling like "Mr. Wall Street," I believe, helps RJ project himself more confidently even during his telephone presentations.

Some salespeople have said, "When in Rome, do as the Romans do"; if your prospects are blue collar workers or farmers, you should be careful not to "overdress." Depending upon what you sell, I disagree. For example, it is understandable for a farm equipment salesperson to dress in bib overalls because, on occasion, a demonstration of an automatic milking machine necessitates his walking in barns knee-high in cow dung. However, other salespeople are not exposed to activities that get their clothes dirty, so they should not dress in casual attire. This "dressing down" when it isn't necessary can be insulting to the very people with whom a salesman is trying to identify. This is particularly true with those selling such products as financial services and insurance policies. These salespeople need to project a highly professional image, one with stability, with which all prospects can relate, regardless of their occupation. And remember: your objective is to gain respect, not win friends.

I don't believe in excessive jewelry, heavy makeup, and large doses of perfume. Women should also avoid dressing in too provocative a manner. Overkill is distracting as well as unprofessional. Sunglasses should only be worn in the sun, and smoking will almost certainly offend most buyers. When in doubt, be conservative.

While the clothes you wear are the most visual and immediate way to create a winning image, owning expensive automobiles, fine art, and luxurious office furnishings, and entertaining customers at your prestigious club generate similar results. Having a high profile in the community by participating in civic and charitable activities also serves to your advantage while making sales calls. Certainly a reputation as an active participant in your area will provide you with some added clout during your approach.

If you have impressive credentials, don't be shy about discussing them. For example, a life insurance agent might begin his presentation by saying: "Before I begin, Fred, let me tell you a little about myself. First, following my degree in finance at Dartmouth and receiving my MBA from Wharton, I began my career as a life underwriter with John Hancock. I've been in the business for eighteen years, and I am a CLU, a member of the National Association of Life Underwriters, and I've been a member of my company's President's Club for the past fourteen years." Here, the salesman is informing the customer that he is a professional and an expert in his field, Furthermore, it is unlikely that a person with this kind of experience will leave the business. He is telling the prospect that he is a lifetime career agent and will be around to provide service.

After a telephone conversation with a prospect during which you set up an appointment, send him this type of information. I suggest that you mention your credentials in a letter, or perhaps include them in a brochure along with some news clippings about your career. The objective is to presell your prospects and make them believe in your ability to serve them. By doing so, you can establish credibility before giving your actual sales presentation.

You Must Do Your Homework

I cannot overemphasize the importance of preparation before the sale. It is presumptuous to walk into somebody's office without having done your homework. When you don't know your facts, you waste both the prospect's time and yours. It borders on rudeness and is insulting to buyers. A lack of preparation is unprofessional and inexcusable.

During the preparation of my manuscript. *Honda: An American Success Story,* I spent hundreds of hours at the Honda manufacturing plant in Marysville, Ohio. Often, while waiting in the lobby, I watched salespeople approach the receptionist and ask questions such as: "Who could I see to

sell paint?" or "I'm with Real Steel Company, and I'd like to
see whoever is in charge of the stamping division." This basic
information is easily gathered before making a sales call. A
telephone call prior to the visit is all that is necessary.

Some salespeople would so flagrantly mispronounce the
names of Honda's Japanese managers that even the managers
themselves were not aware that they were the party being
sought. At the very least, a salesperson should learn the correct pronunciation of a prospect's name and, if necessary,
practice so he can properly say it.

In Japan, a common custom is to immediately identify oneself with a business card; the card is handed sideways to
permit the recipient to read it. Unless an American specifically knows this etiquette in advance, he immediately starts
off on the wrong foot.

The Japanese refrain from making body contact in public;
they are not demonstrative (i.e. no bear hugging or patting
on backs) as are other nationalities, such as the Latin Americans. Here too, I noticed the dismay of Japanese managers
when salespeople failed to recognize even this most elemen-
tary of Japanese customs. I was appalled by this lack of pre-
paredness; clearly the salespeople should have anticipated
meeting with Japanese managers and made an effort to learn
the rudimentary etiquette of how to extend a proper saluta-
tion. Basic courtesy like this should be well researched and
rehearsed, especially when there is an obvious cultural difference.

Of course, doing your homework goes much further than
knowing how to greet someone from a foreign country. In
the case of a large corporation such as Honda, some brushing
up on the company itself is essential. If no other source is
available, try browsing at your local library to find a few
current newspaper and magazine articles. Generally, annual
reports are available at security firms, libraries, or the com-

pany itself, and these, too, should be reviewed. When possible, seek out representatives of firms not in direct competition with what you sell. Certainly they can give you some extra tips before you make your initial call. Not only does being equipped with this type of knowledge demonstrate your professionalism, but it provides you with added confidence—both vital qualities for hardball selling.

In Chapter 3, I mentioned that I ghostwrote a best-selling book for a renowned businesswoman. What I didn't explain was the condition I had to meet before winning the job. Now I'll tell you the rest of the story.

She told me that three women had previously started to write her biography but each had been fired.

"I understand," I replied. "But this time you will be working with me. I sense a certain chemistry between us that exists between a man and a woman and that will make an important difference."

While I wasn't really sure that there was such a difference, she accepted my statement on the condition that I would write an outline of the book and a sample chapter. From this writing, she would judge my capability to write the manuscript. We agreed to meet for a two-hour interview session the following week during which time I could collect the necessary material. However, in order to conduct a thorough interview, I asked for and received a few dozen in-depth magazine and newspaper articles about her. I then painstakingly scrutinized each article in preparation for the interview.

During my session with her, I would ask a question and she would pause to think about her answer. Often, before she could come up with a response, I would give a reply that I thought would be her response. Finally, she exclaimed: "This is amazing. I never met anyone in my life who thought so much as I do. You are definitely the perfect author for my book."

While I did write a fine book and she did receive what had been agreed upon (in the long run, you must provide substance), this is not the point I wish to make here. Rather, I am emphasizing that I did my homework so thoroughly that I knew exactly how the woman would answer—because I asked her questions that I know she would answer as she had in previous interviews. After all, a person doesn't have a different answer each time he or she is asked a specific question. All I had to do was wait until she took a short pause to collect her thoughts; then I would complete her sentence. It was not that we thought so much alike; it was just that I had done my homework!

Some have said that I overprepare for important interviews. They accuse me of spending too much time researching my clients. I disagree. I do my homework so thoroughly that my confidence level soars. Then in the actual presentation, I assume the sale because I am well informed about the other party's needs and what I can do to fulfill those needs. I also believe that no other salesperson, *nobody,* could possibly be better prepared than I. This, I believe, gives me a tremendous edge over any competition.

Admit When You Have Erred

"To err is human," wrote Shakespeare, but to admit it is difficult. A hardball salesperson quickly admits when he has made a mistake; doing so minimizes the damage. The longer one waits to admit an error, the more one's credibility dwindles. It is vital to be the bearer of bad news before the customer hits you with it squarely between the eyes. As long as you must be the bearer of bad news, make it work to your advantage. Otherwise, you get hurt doubly by it—first, by having something go wrong, and second, by losing your credibility. If your client is the one to discover a faux pas, you are put on the defensive; it appears as though you were covering up.

Some historians believe that Richard Nixon would have retained the presidency if he had confessed to having made a mistake when Watergate first surfaced. What would have happened in that case will never be known. However, it is always better to admit up front when you have erred rather than waiting until the error is revealed by somebody else.

Hardball salespeople can turn an error or miscalculation to their advantage.

- A stockbroker calls a client to inform him that the quarterly earnings of Appalachian Industries is 30 percent lower than had originally been projected. There is no point in denying what will soon be publicly announced. It is far better for the broker to personally inform the client that estimated earnings were lower than his expectations. The client can then quickly review his options.

- A computer salesperson must inform a customer that his company cannot install a computer system until the week of May 14th, two months later than originally scheduled, because of a shipping error. He then should offer suggestions for the intervening two months, demonstrating a real concern for the client's business.

- Upon taking a physical examination for a large life-insurance policy, the applicant is informed by the agent that her blood pressure is high. The agent must now tell her that the policy will be rated, increasing her premium by 25 percent. At the same time, he informs the applicant of how fortunate she is to get *any* insurance. "People with high blood pressure used to be considered uninsurable," he explains, "and couldn't obtain any life insurance."

In each of these cases, the salesperson gains respect and exhibits concern by speaking openly rather than ignoring the problem. By his being direct, the problem becomes less threatening because of the obvious integrity and professionalism shown by the salesperson. To avoid facing issues is cowardly and even borderline dishonest. While customers might not like bad news, they appreciate being told the truth. The salesperson gives the clients confidence that they are doing business with a trustworthy and reliable individual.

Problems rarely go away by themselves. I strongly recommend meeting them head-on before they get blown out of proportion. Admit them and, if possible, suggest alternatives. By doing so, you will gain the respect of your customer, and thereby turn potential disaster into an advantage.

The Ganging-up Technique

An effective way to demonstrate your organization's superiority in providing extraordinary service is by the dispatching of backup people to a prospect's place of business. For instance, a computer company might have a team of technicians accompany a sales representative on a follow-up call. A life insurance agency's CPA might team up with an agent to explain a complicated tax matter to a prospective client. In retail sales, a serviceman might be called in to give a technical explanation of a heating system, or a mechanic from the service department might be asked to explain a new car's carburetion system. In each case, the objective is to exhibit the company's depth which, in turn, can better serve the customer.

Two salespeople, working together as a team, may call on

a prospect. Here, they jointly give sales presentations, each doing the part that he or she does best. This can be effective when two areas of expertise are needed. A word of caution, however: If the prospect feels as though it's two-against-one, he may become leary and withdraw. Also, it can be difficult to establish the rapport that comes during a one-to-one presentation. For this reason, I advise that one salesperson maintain a low profile and have minimum participation, allowing his partner to maintain contact.

When presentations are made to a group, a team of two or three salespeople is often appropriate, especially to bolster your position at the conference table. For instance, a salesperson may be at a disadvantage when sitting across the table from a group of ten people brought in to participate in the buying of a computer system. Here, you can avoid *them* ganging up on you by bringing in members of *your* team. It is not that a top salesperson cannot sell a group of people; however, another salesperson accompanying him can back him up and serve as an assistant by answering individual questions without interrupting the entire group.

Ganging up is an effective method if there is a reason, obvious to the client, to do so.

The Out-of-Town Expert

A local salesperson enjoys the advantage of being there to serve the customer *after* the sale. Since this edge is so apparent, there is no need to expand on this thought. Instead, this discussion will focus on how to take advantage of out-of-town status.

In the consulting field, it has been said that an expert is the guy from the next town. While the greater the distance one travels to make a sales call does not, in fact, increase one's knowledge, a hardball salesperson capitalizes on this misconception. I have often used it to my advantage.

First, in the initial contact with the gatekeeper via the telephone, I am sure to emphasize: "This is Robert Shook from Columbus, Ohio, and I'd like to speak to Mr. Clint Eastman." As a general rule, I get put right through, and the greater the distance from my hometown, the less likely it is that I will be asked to give additional information about the nature of my call. The tendency for many gatekeepers is to spend less time cross-examining the out-of-town caller because, like many people, they are conditioned to avoid unnecessary conversation when talking long-distance. To a lesser extent, the same applies to setting up an appointment; it is easier when done long-distance.

On an in-person cold call, I always let the gatekeeper know that I have traveled a long distance to see the prospect. The purpose is to make the call look more important. I never hesitate to mention something like, "I have a four-forty plane to catch," making a quick glance at my watch. Evidently this affectation reduces a gatekeeper's cross-examination because the general response is to expedite getting me into the prospect's office, sometimes ahead of other salespeople also waiting their turn. It is remarkable how often a local salesperson will hear my conversation and say, "Oh, if he's from out of town, I don't mind waiting." (Boy, does he ever need to read *Hardball!*) And I am willing to be obliging and take his turn.

Another edge that the out-of-towner has is people's inclination to think that the further the distance one travels to make a sales call, the more successful he must be. This is based on the belief that a large amount of money is necessary for travel expenses. For example, I know a highly successful group insurance agent who will travel anywhere in the continental United States to make a sales presentation. He believes that the few hundred dollars spent is worth it since he only calls on large corporations and each sale generates five- or six-figure commissions. Yet it is unlikely that a struggling salesperson would be willing to incur these expenses. In some respect, there *is* justification in equating travel with success.

The out-of-town salesperson also creates a sense of urgency by making prospects think it is an imposition to request that he call back. A hardball salesperson is well aware of this edge and doesn't hesitate to use it. "There is no reason why we shouldn't place this order today while I'm in town," he says matter-of-factly.

Planting a Soldier in the Prospect's Camp

I am constantly relying on my background as a salesman to promote my writing career. For instance, a while ago I approached a nationally known business CEO to ghostwrite his book. He had "best-seller" written all over him, and several other writers as well as publishers were actively soliciting him for it. The competition was keen, and my work was cut out for me.

After my initial interview with him, he expressed an interest in two of my previous books by casually saying, "I think these would be good reading material for some of my top managers." While his comment could have easily been dismissed as small talk, I recognized it as just the break I needed.

I grasped the opportunity by saying, "I am so appreciative of the valuable time that you gave me today, I would be delighted and honored to give autographed copies of each book to each member of your management team. I will be insulted if you don't accept them."

He graciously accepted my offer and instructed his personal secretary to give me a list of their names. The list totaled twenty-five key executives, and naturally, I added her name. Signed books were Federal Expressed the following morning.

As I anticipated, my strategy worked brilliantly. I had twenty-five soldiers in his camp who would tell him that my books were wonderful. I knew they would say it even if they couldn't stand them! Why? Because their boss gave the books to them as a gift. What else could they say when he asked how they liked the books! "I thought they were terrible." Not hardly. As the saying goes: Never look a gift horse in the mouth.

In fact, I am sure some of them went out of their way to let him know how much they enjoyed his thoughtful gift. With the twenty-five closest people to the guy giving him feedback that I was an excellent writer, he had to think: "Bob Shook is *the* writer I should have do my autobiography."

I have helped young college graduates get their first jobs with book publishers—again, more Shook soldiers—this time in publishers' camps. I have witnessed leading law firms and Big Eight firms give their blessings to clients who hired attorneys and accountants from their firms. Attorneys and accountants make good soldiers too. And for the same reason, I have witnessed many salespeople give samples of their products to customers' employees. Think about it. I am sure there are many creative ways that you can plant *your* soldiers in customers' camps.

Your Suppliers List

An excellent source of prospects is the people who sell to you. These people are prime candidates. For example, I have talked to stockbrokers just starting their careers, knocking their brains out making cold calls, meanwhile overlooking prospects such as their dentists, doctors, attorneys, clothiers, landlords, and accountants. I am not suggesting that they reduce the number of cold calls they make, but I recommend not passing up anyone who sells goods and services to them.

One life insurance agent confided to me: "If the source from which I buy my office supplies doesn't become my client, I guarantee you that I will find another supplier who will. The same is true with my accountant, attorney, and landlord. Every one of them can be replaced. Why not? Three years ago, I sold a half-million-dollar life policy and a small group health policy to the owner of a fine men's clothing store and he bluntly told me. 'I don't ever expect to see you in a garment that wasn't bought from my store.' He made his point quite clearly and now I buy all my clothes from him." Of course, it's a two-way street. You should expect some requests for reciprocation from those who are your customers too. After all, there are no monopolies on hardball selling.

Wherever you can gain an edge on your competitors, do so. By taking advantage of every opportunity you will feel confident, project the correct image, avoid loss of control of sales situations, and maintain the respect and goodwill of your clients. To reach the level of success that most of us desire, an edge is not a luxury, it's a necessity.

5

Controlling the Sale

Prior to reading this chapter, you must rid yourself of any negative thoughts that controlling the sale connotes manipulating
and browbeating the customer. Hardball selling does not advocate mistreating people nor does it endorse discourtesy.

Some best-selling books suggest various methods of intim-
idating visitors to your office. One such book actually rec-
ommends shortening the legs of the chairs on which your
guests sit. This strategy makes the visitor feel uncomfortable
because he has to look up at you. Another author advises
positioning the office chairs so the guest sits with the sun in
his or her eyes—another technique to evoke discomfort and
retain the upper hand. This sort of one-upmanship is offensive and certainly doesn't build positive, lasting customer
relationships. While it is possible for underhanded tactics to
get a signature on the bottom line, customers are antagonized
and they seldom repeat orders. Keep in mind that a recurring
theme of hardball selling is that a successful sales career is
based on long-term results, not one-time, manipulative tricks.

In some circumstances, there is nothing wrong with an
assumptive close, sometimes referred to as the "either-or"
technique, but it has been used for many years, and I believe

in avoiding clichés. After all, who has not been subjected to a salesperson asking such obvious questions as: "Do you want it delivered to your home or would your office be better?" "Do you prefer the red or blue model?" "Should I put you down for two thousand units or three thousand units?" "Do you want to pay by check or credit card?"

Years ago, Gulf Oil Company's station attendants were instructed to assume the sale by simply saying to each customer: "Fill 'er up with No-Nox?" That's when I concluded that, while the assumptive close is a good one, it is too commonly used to be generally effective. Yet because, under the right circumstances, it *does* get the job done, I am not entirely discounting its application. For this reason, I will discuss it again in Chapter 9, "It's Not Over 'til It's Over." What I do oppose, however, is the use of trite and stereotypical selling methods that tag you as a run-of-the-mill salesperson; being identified as ordinary will automatically strip you of your ability to control the sale.

Controlling the sale is based on four principles of hardball selling that dictate how people tend to procrastinate but do not want to. It is your job to control the sale and guide them to make a buying decision. Your execution must be subtle, however, to have its utmost effect. Nobody likes to be blatantly controlled.

It has been said that there is no such thing as equal control in a relationship between two people; one individual always has more control than the other. In a sales presentation, you need to be that person, because when you lose control, you will likely lose the sale.

The Teacher / Pupil Relationship

A salesperson's job is to educate and motivate the customer to buy his product. Accordingly, the relationship between a salesperson and a customer will resemble that between a teacher and a pupil. If this analogy doesn't suit you, compare your relationship with the customer to that between a parent and child, an officer and enlisted man or woman, a doctor and patient, or a consultant and client.

What common denominator do these relationships share? Each has a first party that exerts control over a second party. However, it is one that is nurturing rather than manipulative. Just as teachers, parents, military officers, doctors, and consultants assume leadership positions, so must you as a salesperson. And like each of them, you must do what is in the best interest of your customer.

Like a teacher, or perhaps a clergyman, a good salesperson receives trust and respect from a customer. And like a pupil or parishioner, so is a customer the recipient of a valuable message, one geared to improve his or her future. As a teacher or clergyman who stands in front of an audience to deliver a lesson, a salesperson delivers his sales presentation. To be effective, the teacher, clergyman, and salesperson must maintain control. Imagine, for instance, the chaos in the classroom of a teacher who didn't have control. Likewise, if your customer takes control of the presentation, your chances of effectively delivering your message and closing the sale are dramatically reduced.

Interestingly, most people are receptive to being put in a nonleadership role. This is true with people from all walks of life. Individuals in power positions who seek needed information will be submissive to a salesperson whom they believe to be an expert in his field. For example, a hard-nosed businessman is told by his physician that to save his life, immediate quadruple bypass surgery is essential; a divorce attorney reads the riot act to his client, a high-powered executive, who is in contempt of court; an auto mechanic explains a complicated engine problem to a Mercedes owner, informing him why a costly repair bill is not under warranty. Clearly, when one is out of his or her field of expertise, he or she has and expects little or no control.

As a hardball salesperson, you are within your rights to assume control of a sales presentation. In this capacity, you are an expert who has the responsibility of conveying important information to the prospect. To properly communicate your message, you must take charge. In fact, the prospect *expects* you to. To do otherwise is shirking your duties as a professional.

Just how effectively a highly successful person can be controlled is demonstrated by the way I did it during an interview I had with W. Clement Stone, the founder and CEO of Combined Insurance Company of America. In 1980, at the time of the interview, he was one of the wealthiest self-made businesspersons in the country.

My purpose for meeting Stone was so I could write a chapter about his career for my book, *The Entrepreneurs.* My objective was to uncover information from him about how he progressed so magnificently from rags to riches. However, I knew beforehand that I would face one major obstacle that might jeopardize the interview. A friend who worked for Stone tipped me off that he had a tendency to ignore the question asked by an interviewer and switch to whatever he felt like talking about. Whenever the subject of his success was discussed, he invariably focused his conversation on a book he coauthored in 1960 with Napoleon Hill titled *Success Through a Positive Mental Attitude.* While the book was an interesting topic, it wasn't what I wanted to write about in *The Entrepreneurs.*

With this knowledge, I spent the first ten minutes of the interview telling him about how I had both a business and writing background. In short, I was selling me, *Robert L. Shook,* to him. Then I plugged in my tape recorder and explained to him that I was planning to record our conversation since it would last approximately two hours and it wasn't possible for me to handwrite accurate notes for such a long period of time.

Before turning on the tape recorder I said: "Mr. Stone, I know that you have been interviewed hundreds of times by reporters who have written about your amazingly successful life. I have done my homework well and have researched these articles. What's more, I read your book, *Success Through a Positive Mental Attitude.* I enjoyed it very much, it was outstanding."

"Thank you," he said appreciatively.

At this point I set the stage to either take complete control over one of the country's most powerful businessmen, or get thrown out on my ear without an interview. I took the risk because I knew that without being in control I would accomplish little talking to him. "Mr. Stone," I said, looking him squarely in the eye, "I have been told that you have a strong tendency to dominate an interview of this nature. No matter what you are asked, you switch the conversation to your book and give the same answers regardless of the interviewer's questions. I have copies of your articles and speeches—and your book. I do not want the same things told to me that have been quoted and requoted by other writers. So, if you start talking about anything that I feel is unrelated to my question, I am simply going to turn off the tape recorder and ask that you stick to my specific question. You might not appreciate my doing this, but if that is what it takes for me to get a fresh interview and write an excellent chapter about you, I am going to do exactly that. Now, if you have any questions you want to ask me before I turn on this tape recorder, please do so."

Stone stared at me as if he could not believe what he had just heard. Then, without any emotion whatsoever, he responded: "Go ahead and turn that thing on." It was a superb interview.

Did he resent my assuming a leadership role? No. He wouldn't have been shy about expressing himself if he had been offended. In fact, I'm sure he admired the way I had taken control—it was a treatment he rarely experienced during an interview. But then, it's doubtful that he had ever come eye to eye with a writer with my hardball selling experience.

Taking Control

If you do not have control in the beginning of a sales relationship, then the prospect does, and you're going to have to take it away from him. The sooner you take control of a sales presentation the better. What you don't want to do is place yourself in a position of weakness and be faced with an uphill battle. To get immediate control, you have to be a take-charge person, but you must be subtle about it. The key is to gain control without being so obvious that you offend people.

In 1975, while writing *Total Commitment*, I set up an appointment to meet with Colonel Harland Sanders of Kentucky Fried Chicken fame. I spoke directly with the colonel and he agreed to pick me up at the airport.

"My flight arrives at nine-fifty-eight on Friday morning," I told him.

"Good," said the colonel. "I'll pick you up at the airport. I won't know who you are, but you'll recognize me."

I eagerly looked forward to meeting Colonel Sanders, a man who had genuinely become a legend in his own time. The plane landed on schedule, and I headed directly to the airport's main entrance where the colonel and his driver would be waiting to pick me up. From there we would go to his home, where we would spend the entire day. I spotted him waiting for me, and it delighted me that everything was going like clockwork.

"Colonel Sanders," I said enthusiastically, extending my hand to greet him. "I'm Robert Shook."

"There ain't gonna be an interview today," the colonel moaned. "I fell on the ice and banged up my head."

"It's a real pleasure to meet you, sir," I continued, paying no attention to his comment about cancelling the interview. "I'm sorry about your accident."

"I fell on the ice this morning and gave myself a good bruise," he continued. "I had no way to contact you to cancel the interview. I didn't want to leave you here at the airport looking for me and me not showing up, so I stopped out here on my way to the doctor."

"That's fine with me, Colonel," I said, still ignoring his attempt to cancel. Unless I did some fast thinking, I had flown down to Louisville for nothing. "I'll go with you, and as soon as we get your bruise treated, we'll head on over to your place."

With that, I turned to the driver and said, "Which way is the car parked?"

"Uh, over there." He pointed.

"Let's get going," I said, and started walking in the direction of the car, "we have to get the colonel to the doctor." The two of them automatically followed me. After the doctor did some minor mending of the colonel's head, we spent the rest of the day doing the interview. By my staying in complete control from start to finish, what nearly turned out to be a disaster was turned into a highly productive day.

I assumed control with the colonel; in an inoffensive way I was able to win him over. A less experienced salesperson might have reacted differently and said: "Look, I flew all the way down here from Columbus, Ohio, to see you and my return flight doesn't depart until seven o'clock this evening. What am I supposed to do for the next nine hours?"

Having had the opportunity to know the colonel, I am sure he would have replied, "That's your problem, not mine. Now

I've got to get to the doctor," and the meeting with him would have ended that instant.

Unless you have a good reason to think differently, a good rule of thumb is to *always* assume that people would rather follow than lead. The numbers support this rule. Look at the followers in this world in comparison to the relatively few leaders, and you will see that the percentage play is to take control of every sale and assume a leadership position.

Anticipation

About three months after meeting Colonel Sanders, I relied on my sales background to get an interview with golfing great Sam Snead.

Snead was the pro at the Greenbrier, the world-class resort in White Sulphur Springs, West Virginia, and I called him to set up a meeting in conjunction with a three-day convention I was attending. He granted me a two-hour interview. "Just stop by the clubhouse when you arrive, and we'll set up a time," he instructed me.

Shortly after I checked in at the front desk, I headed to the clubhouse to see Snead. "My name is Robert Shook," I announced upon entering his office.

Snead was sitting at his desk and replied: "Who?"

"Perhaps you don't recall my name, but I'm Robert Shook, the writer..."

"Writer?"

"I'm here to do an interview with you for my book, *Total Commitment*, the one we spoke about on the telephone. The one that includes twenty great American achievers such as Jesse Owens, Colonel Sanders, Pete Rose, and Kemmons Wilson, who founded Holiday Inn..."

"I don't have the slightest idea what you're talking about," Snead interrupted. "Tell me more about your book."

With this, he started rubbing his fingers together and said: "You know what I mean. I'm talking about the green stuff."

I understood perfectly. He knew all along what I was talking about. I knew that Sam Snead had a reputation for being a golf hustler, and here he was, hustling me to pay him to be in my book.

"Yes, Sam, I know exactly what you mean," I said, reaching into my wallet. A smile flashed on Snead's face. I pulled out a check which I handed to him. It was a check in the amount of one hundred dollars payable to me by Jesse Owens.

He stared and stuttered. "This isn't . . ."

"Hey relax, Sam, I've got some good news for you. I'm not going to charge you anything to be in my book. This interview is on me."

"What's going on? I don't get it . . ."

My face broke out in a big smile and it seemed to put him at ease. "Let me explain," I said. "Last February when I interviewed Jesse Owens at his home in Phoenix, I told him that if he was ever in Columbus to please look me up. This past Tuesday while he was in town for a speaking engagement, he called, and we got together for lunch. While I was driving him back to his hotel, he asked me to stop by a bank so he could cash a check. It was pouring down rain, so I asked him, 'How much cash do you need?'

" 'A hundred bucks,' he said.

"I had the cash on me, so I said, 'There's no sense in getting wet, just make it out to me,' and I handed him the money. This is how I happen to have this check from Jesse Owens. Now, it isn't possible for me to pay all of the high-profile people in *Total Commitment* for their time. However, they still participate because the book is good public relations for them." I paused briefly and seeing that Snead was nodding his head in agreement, I said, "So what's the best time tomorrow morning for an interview that will take approximately two to three hours?"

"How does eight o'clock sharp sound to you, Bob?" he asked good-naturedly.

It was not just a coincidence that I had Jesse Owens's check in my wallet. Normally, I cash personal checks within a day or two. However, while researching Sam Snead, I had read stories about his money-hungry reputation and how he hustled people on and off the golf course. Knowing this, I *anticipated* that this one-hundred-dollar check could possibly be a selling tool to spring on Snead. In fact, during the five-hour drive to the Greenbrier, I rehearsed how I'd use it if Snead asked to be paid for the interview. I anticipated.

It always shocks me when salespeople fail to anticipate even the most obvious curves that are routinely thrown at them. For example, insurance agents have to know that people are going to say, "I'm insurance-poor and not interested in more life insurance." Car salespeople know that there are "tire kickers" who say, "I'll be back to see you after I look around to see what prices the other dealers are offering." And every salesperson has encountered rebuttals such as "I want to think it over," and "I never make a buying decision without first talking to my wife/husband." Salespeople hear these comments too often not to anticipate them.

Yet, while these put-offs are constantly voiced, many salespeople remain unprepared, because they lack a solid, effective way to answer them. It makes sense to anticipate these rebuttals and go in with an arsenal of field-tested comebacks. (See Chapter 7, "Creating a Sense of Urgency.") Regardless of what you sell, there are certain predictable obstacles that, when you are properly prepared, should never interfere with your selling effort. Plus there are those "special" situations, such as my encounter with Sam Snead, when you must tailor-make your presentation to fit the prospect. If you do your homework properly, it's a simple task to anticipate how to ensure a creative approach.

A Forceful Presence

Hardball selling is not for the faint-hearted. You can't tiptoe your way past grilling gatekeepers nor can you timidly approach hard-nosed executives and expect to gain control of a sales presentation. Lessons learned in charm school don't work in the real world of selling.

While I'm not suggesting that you steamroll your way into the prospect's office, you must project a forceful presence. You simply will not control sales presentations without one. And, as previously mentioned, once the buyer has control, you're faced with an uphill battle; it's far better to maintain control from the start.

To accomplish this, you must approach each prospect with self-assurance and a serious demeanor. No matter how cheerful and content you may be, it's inappropriate to walk in with a big smile on your face. Admittedly, it may take some practice to perfect this no-nonsense image, particularly when you're in a cheerful mood after having closed the sale with your last prospect. It's no easy task to hide your happy feelings. However, it's the kiss of death to come across as a friendly, easy-going salesperson; you must appear to be forceful—an attribute that people associate with authority and expertise. The salesperson with the toothy grin and a repertoire of stale warm-up jokes will not be taken seriously. Making prospects laugh does not guarantee sales.

One of the best examples of the necessity of forcefulness I ever witnessed occurred early in my career. An inexperienced, overly friendly agent who worked for our agency returned twenty-five leads at the end of the week with the words "Not interested" written on each of them. The leads were small-business owners on the south side of Pittsburgh.

"I called on every one of these," he complained at a Saturday morning sales meeting, "and none of them are interested in disability insurance. I want a new territory. The people in this section of town are too tough to sell."

My father, Herb Shook, who was my partner, was livid. "Are you suggesting that it's the territory's fault?"

"That's right," the agent argued, "and I refuse to work in this area."

"Give me the lead cards," Herb said, "and I will call on each of them next week. I guarantee you I'll sell ten of them."

It was quite a challenge, considering that the agent had just called on these prospects. I knew my father was trying to impress on the other agents that there is no such thing as a bad territory; but at the same time, I didn't want to see him fail in his attempt to make a point. "Why don't you wait a few weeks," I suggested, "and then do it? Don't you think it's too soon to call on the *same* prospects?"

"No, I'll start on Monday morning," he insisted.

Not a man to renege on his word, Herb called on all twenty-five prospects. Although he was selling the identical policy that the other agent tried to sell the previous week, Herb walked in with a much more forceful approach. "Mr. Prospect," he addressed each of the leads, "my name is Herbert Shook with Shook Associates, and as you recall, one of our new agents was here last week to review a disability insurance policy with you. I understand you had no interest, and I would like to talk to you for a few minutes to find out why you reacted as you did. After all, we have had such a wonderful reception on this long-term disability policy, we want to find out if perhaps our new agent had been negligent in his explanation of its benefits. Let's go into your office where we won't have any disturbances so I can show you what you're *now* eligible for."

Without waiting for a reply, Herb assumed that the prospect was interested and headed straight toward the office. He was able to give presentations to twenty-three out of the twenty-five NG ("no good") leads. Every time he explained a feature, he'd preface it by saying, "Now this is *very important,* so I want you to listen very carefully." And every now and then he'd emphasize, "Pay close attention to this because I am quite certain you might have overlooked it last week and you are going to really appreciate it." He would even ask, "Do you see how terrific this feature is?"

"Yes, I can see you're right," a prospect would say.

"Boy, I'll say. This is great," another would comment.

He would also stress, "This is a brand-new feature that businesspeople are very excited about," and after his explanation, he'd add, "Isn't that terrific?" And each time, the response was, "I'll say. That *is* quite a difference."

Herb proved his point: There was no such thing as a poor territory. He sold seventeen out of the twenty-five prospects *selling the identical policy they had all rejected the previous week!* He also demonstrated that a forceful, no-nonsense presence does, indeed, get results.

Fact-finding

Many salespeople share the erroneous belief that each time a prospect is permitted to voice an opinion, it's possible that he could take control from them. This thinking dictates that selling is a one-way conversation—the seller talks and the buyer listens. It also suggests that when a buyer is allowed to speak, he might talk about an unrelated subject or, worse, voice a objection. Notwithstanding, hardball selling advocates two-way communication, and unless the buyer is actively engaged in the conversation, a salesperson operates under a severe handicap. When the seller encourages the

Controlling the Sale

buyer to participate, important thoughts are expressed, and in turn, vital feedback is provided.

As the name implies, fact-finding is a question-and-answer session conducted by a salesperson to seek vital information necessary to create the need for a product. When properly handled, control of the sale is not in jeopardy; on the contrary, it is increased. Note, for example, that a teacher doesn't lose control by quizzing a classroom of students, nor does a trial attorney lose it by cross-examining a witness. Likewise, a salesperson can maintain control while simultaneously permitting a prospect to participate in a fact-finding session.

Although some salespeople view the fact-finding segment of a sales presentation as a drilling session, when correctly executed, it isn't offensive to the prospect. Instead, it's considered professional and authoritative. Observe, for example, the positive manner in which you react to a doctor during an examination:

"When did you first begin to notice it?"
"What were you doing at the time?"
"Tell me what it feels like."
"Is it a sharp pain or a constant pain?"
"Exactly where does it hurt?"
"How about if I press right here?"
"Does it hurt more when you stand up?"
"Does it feel better when you're sitting or lying in a prone position?"
"How do you feel after a big meal?"

The doctor continues to question the patient until he is able to make a proper diagnosis. Then he says, "Based on what you have told me, I am going to recommend ..."

Do people resent the doctor's questioning? Not in the least. On the other hand, imagine a doctor who doesn't bother to

101

ask questions and right off the bat says, "It hurts right here. Okay, I'm going to do some cutting." It's highly probable that the patient will seek another opinion.

Under similar circumstances, a good CPA cross-examines his client before making any recommendations about tax-saving strategies; a business consultant conducts a lengthy session to collect the facts he needs prior to presenting a business plan; a divorce attorney gathers his facts before he offers his advice. In each of these scenarios, a professional asks many questions and allows the client to speak freely, while, at the same time, always maintaining control. Furthermore, nobody considers it to be offensive when a cross-examiner pries for information. Instead, it is appreciated. It demonstrates a caring attitude and a concern for details that has a positive influence on the sale.

The doubting Thomases are quick to point out that a doctor, CPA, consultant, and attorney are not salespeople. "A salesperson's role is different," they stress. "Prospects are suspicious about his motives so he cannot conduct a fact-finding session with the same degree of professionalism." While this may be true of the majority of salespeople, a truly professional salesperson operates on a higher level and, as a consequence, is given the same respect as the nonselling professionals. For example:

A stockbroker asks: "What are your financial objectives?"
"What are your short-term and long-term objectives?"
"What do you want to achieve with your investments?"
"Are you interested in capital gains or income?"
"What do you consider to be a good yield?"
"How do you feel about tax-free municipals?"
"How do you feel about the so-called glamor stocks selling at high multiples?"

"Tell me about some of your past investments."

"What is the approximate value of your present portfolio?"

"How liquid are you?"

"What is your present net worth?"

A real estate broker asks: "Do you own your present home?"

"What is its approximate value?"

"How much equity do you have in it?"

"Tell me about your family."

"What are the ages of your children?"

"How important is the school district where you want to live?"

"What price range are you interested in?"

"What kind of home do you want? A one-story or a two-story?"

"What style home? A colonial, contemporary, ranch, or Tudor?"

"Is a large yard an important consideration?"

"Do you like newer homes or older homes?"

"Is it important to live close to your job?"

"Is good public transportation a factor?"

"If you could find your 'dream' home, what is the highest price you would consider paying for it?"

"What is your timetable for buying a new home?"

A life insurance agent asks: "How much insurance do you now have?"

"What is your date of birth?"

"Tell me about your health."

"Tell me about your family."

"What do you do for a living?"

"What fringe benefits does your company provide?"

"What do you think about life insurance as an investment versus pure protection (term)?"

"What have you done to provide for your children's
education?"

"What plans have you made for your financial security
after you retire?"

"What is your approximate net worth?"

"Are you familiar with how much estate taxes your heirs
would be obligated to pay based on the size of your present
estate?"

As you can see, the above questions are indeed similar to
the ones asked by professionals in nonselling fields. Additionally, they provide essential information. Imagine a stockbroker who never asked questions, but instead started his sales
presentation with a new client by saying: "I recommend that
you buy five thousand shares of Widget International, which
is currently selling at forty dollars a share." Or upon first
meeting a prospective home buyer, a real estate broker who
said: "I have a six-thousand-square-foot house in the far north
side of town I want to show you." Or a life insurance agent
who never asked any questions but instead said: "I recommend that you take out a million-dollar policy." Is there any
difference here from the doctor who says: "You say it hurts
right here. Well, then I'll have to cut"?

Dorothy Leeds, the president of Organizational Technologies, Inc., a management and sales consulting firm, says: "The
main reasons questions are so effective is that most people
love to answer them. Questions stimulate the mind and
offer people an opportunity to use their brains construc-
tively."

Leeds, the author of *Smart Questions: A New Strategy for
Successful Managers,* emphasizes: "One of the axioms of hu-

man communications is that most people prefer talking to listening. When you ask for someone's thoughts and opinions, you give him an opportunity to talk." She also explains: "Hearing a question puts the listener on the alert. The phrasing and cadence instantly let him know he's expected to do more than listen; he's expected to respond." A well-conducted fact-finding session does exactly this, and at the same time, allows you to maintain control. As an added bonus, vital information about the prospect is also revealed.

As James Thurber said: "It is better to know some of the questions than to know all of the answers."

Let the Buyer Participate

The more the buyer participates, the more you have control. When someone is concentrating on what you're selling, it's difficult for him to be thinking about something else. This means the prospect is not thinking about his golf game, his redheaded secretary, or for that matter, how else he would rather spend his money.

Here too, you assume the teacher role, with the buyer placed appropriately in the pupil role. When you instruct the buyer, step by step, how to operate anything from a clock radio to a computer, you are in the driver's seat. During a properly executed demonstration the salesperson actually gives the buyer a series of small orders that are, in turn, obediently followed. It works like this:

"Have you ever worked one of these before? Let me show you."

"Okay, now, just push this button. No, like this. Okay, try it again."

"Now come over here and try this."

"Okay. Now do it again."

"Okay, this time I want you to do it completely on your own."

Do you see how effectively it works? While you are not actually talking down to the prospect (which is offensive), you are taking complete charge of the presentation during the demonstration; the prospect is so involved in his role as a participant, he never objects.

Recently I bought a new suit, and it wasn't until I got home that evening that I realized how I was totally controlled by the salesman. And he did it by getting me to participate. The salesman gave a series of small orders, and as a little boy innocently obeys his teacher, I did exactly what I was instructed to do.

He picked a suit off the rack and said, "I think you'll look good in this suit. Try it on in the dressing room."

I hesitated slightly, which prompted him to say: "Over there. The dressing room is through that door."

I came out of the dressing room and headed toward him on the other side of the department. Dragging through the store with the pants and sleeves covering my extremities, I realized what Dopey must have felt like in *Snow White and the Seven Dwarfs*. "Over here." The salesman beckoned. "I want the tailor to measure you in front of this mirror."

Again, I did as I was instructed. "Face looking in *that* mirror," he told me. "And stand up straight."

"Let your arm drop naturally."

"Turn sideways."

"Don't move."

"Do you like your coat sleeve length just past your shirtsleeve?"

"You don't? I do, and that's how I think you should wear it."

In the meantime, the tailor kept putting chalk marks all over the suit. Both of them had obviously assumed that I was going to buy the garment, although I never said so. They assumed it because I never said *I wasn't going to buy* when the salesman gave me all of those little orders that I obediently followed. By the time the suit was completely covered with chalk marks for alteration, I would have felt very foolish saying, "Well, thanks for letting me try on the suit, but I'm just browsing around."

"Okay that's it," he finally said. "You look terrific. Now go back to the dressing room and after you get dressed in your other clothes, bring your *new* suit back to me. I'll wait here for you."

Although I initially walked in the store to buy some shirts and was, in fact, just browsing in the suit department when I was approached by the salesman. I'm not complaining. I needed a new suit. I'm not a shopper, so I *needed* a take-charge salesman to sell it to me. He was able to get me to participate by giving me a series of small orders—it worked like a charm.

Getting the Customer to Open Up

Some people aren't talkers, and it's sometimes difficult to get them to participate in the sales interview. These buyers have to be drawn into the conversation. Although it's easy to dominate the conversation and not let them get a word in edgewise, you must open them up so they will express their needs. There are several ways to accomplish this, and, at the same time, control the sale.

Sometimes this is accomplished by simply asking an opinion question, such as : "How do you feel about ..." "Tell me what you had in mind ..." "How does this philosophy coincide with yours?" Questions of this nature require more than a yes or no response. However, if that is all you get, pause for a few seconds; usually, the buyer will break the silence by giving a more detailed answer.

Most people view a silence in a conversation as a void. It's

not, and you should never feel uncomfortable when one occurs. Furthermore, when a buyer has voiced his opinion, it
isn't necessary for you to speak immediately. Sometimes, remaining quiet, instead of taking your turn in the dialogue, will
lead the other party to reveal an astonishing amount of information. Don't worry about making people feel ill at ease
by remaining silent. I have *never* heard anyone criticize a
salesperson for this reason.

Of course, when you're not talking, it gives you time to
regroup and collect your thoughts. When I was in Japan, I
observed how the Japanese businessmen, who spoke otherwise good English, used translators. It took me a while to
catch on before I realized that this permitted them more time
to think through what they wanted to say. Use this "quiet
time" to think through your strategy for closing the sale.

Jeff Slutsky, founder and president of Retail Marketing In-
stitute, a consulting group in Columbus, Ohio, has a technique he calls the "echo" that he uses during fact-finding
sessions. Slutsky insists that it is possible for a salesperson to
learn only by listening, not talking. With this in mind, he
believes that by keeping the prospect talking, you will eventually find out everything you need to know to solve his
problems and close the sale.

"The 'echo' technique simply takes the last few words of
whatever the client says and repeats those words in the form
of a question," explains Slutsky. "Then shut up and let the
client volunteer more and more details.

"For example, a client might say, 'We're looking for a way
to increase our sales on the local level.'

"You respond by saying, 'Local level?'

" 'Yeah, you see, we're already doing as much as we can
with our national budget, so we need something that will
enhance what we're already doing.'

" 'Already doing?'

" 'Sure. We're spending about five percent of sales now on our advertising and we feel we should be getting a bigger return.'

" 'Bigger return?' "

As you can see, the secret is to encourage the prospect to talk by asking brief questions relative to his comments. By asking quick, specific questions that are followed up with silence while he speaks, you can control the conversation. Furthermore, this technique is unlikely to be detected because the prospect is too involved in concentrating on his responses.

Here's a good rule to remember about asking questions: Never ask a question you don't want to hear the answer to. Or, to put it another way, avoid opening a can of worms if you aren't going fishing. For example, if a customer has had a bad experience with your company and you are aware of his temper tantrums when the subject is brought up, for goodness sake, don't ask him to tell you about it.

A good tip to remember about asking questions to get a response from the prospect: If the customer makes a remark that you don't like, respond with the question, "Why are you saying that?" For instance, a life insurance agent might ask this question of a prospect who says: "I'm insurance-poor." A stockbroker might ask it of a customer who says: "I won't touch a company that's not listed on the Big Board." "Why are you saying that?" is a thought-provoking question that any salesperson can ask—and you can ask it of the same customer several times if necessary.

Give Other People Credit for Your *Idea*

Years ago, my wife, Bobbie, and I received a dinner invitation from an editor with Harper & Row whom I had never previously met. It was supposed to be strictly a social get-together; however, I was anxious to sell a manuscript I was contemplating writing. I had tentatively titled it, "Ten Super Sales-persons." On the way to the restaurant, I discussed the book's concept with my wife and told her: "Watch how I sell it to him. I'm going to make him think my idea is his idea." My strategy was based on two points. First, I had heard he had a big ego, and second, I understood that "people will support those things which they help to create."

During the course of the dinner, we briefly discussed my writing career, which, in 1978, included three published books; however, I mostly discussed my real career, which was being employed full-time as a sales executive. I focused the conversation on my selling experience to impress him with my expertise on the subject of the book that I was about to propose.

When we started talking about books, I casually mentioned: "The majority of books about selling are based on a single writer's opinion. I think salespeople would love to read a book that expressed several leading salespeople's opinions."

"Are you suggesting that the book be coauthored by several salespeople?" he asked.

"That would be a good idea except it would be difficult to implement," I commented.

"Yes, and it would be hard to find top salespeople with writing skills."

"That would definitely be a problem," I said.

"No, one writer could interview leading salespeople and do profiles on them."

"That would be terrific," I said. "What do you think would be the best way to select who would be in the book?"

"You could pick the top salesperson in different fields. You know, the top car salesman, the number one life insurance agent, the best stockbroker," he volunteered.

"What about identifying the top salesperson with leading companies like IBM and Xerox?" I added.

"Good idea," he said.

"What do you suppose would be an ideal number to include? Five? Eight? Ten?" I asked.

"Ten would be perfect," he said.

"We could call it, 'The Ten Best Salesmen.' "

"You can't use salesmen," he corrected me. " 'The Ten Best Salespersons.' The book has to profile at least two women with today's women's lib movement."

"Absolutely," I agreed. "What do you think about 'Ten Super Salespersons'?"

"I don't like the word 'super,' " he said. "What do you think about 'Greatest,' Bob?"

" 'Ten Greatest Salespersons,' I love it. Salespeople all over the country will love this book."

"You have an excellent background for this," he said enthusiastically. "Would you consider authoring it?"

"Well," I said hesitantly, and with that, my wife gave me a pinch under the table.

"I'd like to work with you on it, Bob," he said.

"It would be fun to work with an idea man like you," I replied. "Okay, shake. It's a deal."

We shook hands and I wrote the book. And in case you're interested, it's still in print.

Intensity

Listen to a sports announcer describing an all-Pro NFL linebacker: "Number thirty-six is playing with incredible intensity." Interestingly, many of the league's leading linebackers are not the fastest or the biggest players on the field. Yet, in spite of this, they excel as a result of their total concentration on every play in every game. The same is true of a championship boxer who never lets up and relentlessly hammers away at his opponent. These athletes give their complete concentration to their efforts; they are never distracted by the roar in the stadium or the millions of viewers glued to their television sets.

In the same way, nature's great hunters will stalk their prey with full intensity. Instinctively, the predators focus on their kill by blocking out all distractions that might interfere with their single purpose. The hunters' survival rests on their ability to maintain intensity.

Intensity is also an essential ingredient in the jungle of hardball selling. You, too, must devote your full, undivided attention to each sale, not allowing distractions to throw you off course. Yet, all too often, I have observed salespeople allowing their eyes to wander at the least diversion, which is likely to be picked up by the prospect. What do you think a customer is thinking when your eyes are wandering to your watch, or worse yet, his pretty daughter? Or when you're listening to a nearby conversation during a luncheon meeting? This behavior relays a nonverbal message signaling that you have little concern about his welfare. You must make eye contact with the prospect and never allow your eyes to wander. The more intensely you focus on him, the more you will control the sales presentation. When you lose your concentration, you are also apt to lose control.

As a side note, it always appalls me when I see salespeople in a retail store, who, in front of a customer, take telephone calls and engage in lengthy conversations with callers. A phone customer should never be given priority over someone who took the time to come to the store.

Taking Abuse Is Not Part of Your Job Description

A hardball salesperson does not take abuse from anyone, and when he is harassed by a customer, he dishes it right back. It's not that he can't take it; instead, he understands that each time anyone takes a beating without putting up a fight, a small toll is paid. These experiences slowly destroy one's self-esteem.

An effective way to maintain control is to assume the offensive stance whenever placed in a defensive position. When a comparison between Dan Quayle and John F. Kennedy was brought up during the nationally televised vice presidential debates in 1988, a striking difference between the two men surfaced: the style in which they fielded news commentators' questions. For example, Tom Brokaw asked Dan Quayle to explain what was the first thing he would do upon assuming the presidency, and the vice presidential candidate replied that he would pray. Brokaw was not satisfied that praying was a solid answer, so again he asked the question, and then a third time. Each time, Quayle gave what many observers believed were weak answers, and no one was impressed. Had Brokaw been around during the 1960 Kennedy-Nixon debates, he would never have gotten away with asking Kennedy the same question a second time. Had Brokaw done so, Kennedy would have shaken his finger at him and firmly said: "I answered that question once before, and I refuse to go into that subject again." Like a seasoned hardball salesperson, Kennedy spoke with authority and conviction; the American voters loved it.

Buck Rodgers, IBM's legendary vice president of marketing, tells a story about the time he flew to Chicago to accompany a group of IBMers on a sales call. They were meeting with the president of a multibillion-dollar corporation at 10 A.M. "We arrived right on time," Rodgers explains, "and were ushered into a reception room outside his office. His secretary said he'd be right with us, and we sat there for a half hour. At ten-thirty, I said to my people. 'We've waited long enough. Let's go.'

"That afternoon, the president of the company called me.

'Hey Buck, I thought we had an appointment this morning,' he said.

" 'We did.'

" 'Where were you?'

" 'We were there.'

" 'I didn't see you.'

" 'That's because we left at ten-thirty.'

" 'Why did you do that?' he asked.

" 'Because we had a ten o'clock meeting, and that's what time we were there. But you kept us waiting. There is no reason for IBMers to be treated that way.'

"The president apologized and we rescheduled the appointment for the following morning," Rodgers said. "This meeting started exactly on time, and it was a good one."

Had Rodgers submitted to his customer's abuse, he would undoubtedly have lost control. By refusing to do so, he was able to deal with the president of a multibillion-dollar corporation on equal footing.

It doesn't matter who the customer is—an old lady who comes into a dealership showroom to buy a car, or the CEO of an international corporation—a hardball salesperson always stays in control of the sale. By doing it in a polite but firm manner, nobody is offended—and, for the most part, the customer appreciates it.

The Bigger the Sale, the Bigger the Commission

When asked why he robbed banks, Willie Sutton, the notorious bank robber, replied, "Because that's where the money is." Salespeople who sell on a straight commission basis would do well to share this thinking and concentrate on prosperous prospects with the wherewithal to place substantial orders.

It's a poor percentage play to use valuable time and energy calling on prospects who, at best, have marginal resources. Realistically, no matter how great a need and desire you create for your product, a sale cannot be closed when there is no money to finance it. Under this scenario, the four principles of hardball selling are not applicable because no matter how much high pressure is applied, subtle or otherwise, you can't get blood out of a stone.

Going for the Big Ones

Some salespeople have a tendency to shy away from the biggest and most affluent prospects. Their anxiety often stems from a lack of confidence; salespeople can feel uncomfortable, or perhaps even inferior, in the presence of powerful and influential individuals. While I cannot offer a psychological explanation of why such behavior exists, it is, nevertheless, a factor that adversely influences one's selling output.

It is therefore essential to emphasize that you must not avoid calls on any qualified prospects in your territory, and most important, never rule out anyone who appears "overqualified." To do so is to turn over to your competition your prime business opportunities. You might as well hand him your commission checks. Hardball selling champions thinking big, always going for the biggest prizes. You must never shortchange yourself by putting an artificial cap on your potential earning power.

Big Prospects Are People Too

A common misconception is that highly successful people are imposing, heavy-handed, and self-willed. Prior to authoring *The Chief Executive Officers*, I, too, had my own preconceived notions. In 1980, when I conducted a series of interviews with Americans who headed giant corporations, I anticipated meeting self-centered, egotistical individuals. My apprehension was based on images generated by the media, not ones from personal exposure to people in positions of immense power and influence. In preparation for writing my manuscript, I interviewed ten of the nation's business leaders who were the CEOs of the following companies: American Express, American Telephone & Telegraph, Avon Cosmetics, Federated Department Stores, E. I. du Pont Nemours & Company, General Motors, General Electric, Gulf Oil, Prudential Insurance Company of America, and UAL, Inc.

After spending several hours in meetings with each of these CEOs, I realized how different they were from what I had expected. I discovered success doesn't ruin people but instead enhances them. I share the sentiments expressed by Somerset Maugham, who said: "The common idea that success spoils people by making them vain, egotistical and self-complacent is erroneous; on the contrary, it makes them, for the most part, humble, tolerant, and kind. Failure makes people bitter and cruel."

I have learned that an individual who comes from a humble background doesn't change for the worse as he climbs the ladder of success. For example, a person who is thoughtful and sensitive in his twenties doesn't lose these caring attributes when promoted to a high-level management position in his forties or fifties. While people's careers and lifestyles change, the basic qualities they possess remain the same.

Interestingly, during the course of my meetings with these chief executives, I observed that the best-managed corporations develop their top management from within. My research revealed that it is a sign of a firm's weakness when it must go to the outside and bring in high-ranking managers from other organizations. It's a clear message that the company doesn't have the capability to effectively groom its own people. The low entry levels at which several of these men began their careers attest that the cream does indeed rise to the top in a well-managed organization. For instance, Avon's CEO, David Mitchell, started as a mailroom clerk; Robert Beck was first hired as an insurance agent and worked his way through the ranks to become Prudential's chairman of the board; Thomas Murphy, CEO of General Motors, began his career with the company as an accounting clerk; AT&T's Charles Brown first worked in equipment maintenance and had twenty-three different positions before being named chairman of the board; Richard Ferris was initially hired to operate a grill in a hotel of a subsidiary company of UAL. Seventeen years later, at age forty-two, he was elected chief executive officer of the giant airline and lodging conglomerate.

People are people and hardball selling methods are equally effective regardless of one's social or economic status. Highly successful people are no different from anyone else. They are ordinary people who have achieved extraordinary accomplishments. To contradict F. Scott Fitzgerald, rich people are just like anyone else except they have more money. A salesperson should never stereotype them and think they require a separate set of selling tactics.

The four principles of hardball selling do not discriminate. I have met with many of the nation's most successful people, so I can say with authority that the selling techniques espoused in this book work with high-profile people.

A case in point is well illustrated by a meeting I had with Edgar Speer, who, at the time, served as the CEO of U.S. Steel, the world's largest steel company. My coauthor, Ron Bingaman, and I were sitting across the desk from Speer, doing a tape-recorded interview for our book, *Total Commitment*. Suddenly, Ron looked at his watch and said: "Say, Bob, look what time it is. It's three-twenty. We're already twenty minutes over the one-hour interview we told Mr. Speer we'd conduct."

Before the dynamic steel executive could reply, I gave Ron a swift kick under the table and asked a question on which Speer elaborated for quite some time. I continued to drill him and he continued to talk, seemingly without regard for the time of day. Once more Ron broke in: "Look at the time," he exclaimed. "It's four-thirty. We've taken up an hour and a half more of Mr. Speer's time than we said we would!"

With that, I flicked off the tape recorder and, turning to my coauthor, said in a harsh voice: "Mr. Speer is a big boy, and I am sure he knows what time it is. If he wants us to leave, he's not too bashful to say so." I turned the tape recorder back on and said, "And now if we may continue with our interview, sir ..." An ear-to-ear grin appeared on Speer's face and he gave me a wink. He then continued to answer every question until the interview was completed, over two hours later than had been scheduled.

Although my coauthor was a fine writer, he was not a salesperson; plus, he was intimidated by Speer's position. Consequently, he didn't realize that the interview with Speer could be controlled in the same way that I had done it for so many years while conducting fact-finding sessions a a salesman. Furthermore, Ron didn't realize that although a prospect grants x amount of time to hear out a sales presentation, it is permissible to exceed the scheduled time frame when no resistance is offered.

Once you get the hang of it, hardball selling becomes second nature and neither the prospect *nor* you will be consciously aware of it. Eventually, it becomes automatic—with everyone. This became obvious to me when I interviewed Ralph Lazarus, who, at the time, was the CEO of Federated, the largest department store chain in the U.S. My morning meeting was initially scheduled for two hours, beginning at ten o'clock at his Cincinnati offices. I didn't pay a lot of attention to the time, but I do remember it was 3:30 when I left.

It was not until that evening when I listened to the taped interviews that I realized there were more than four hours of recorded conversation. In fact, around the two-and-a-half-hour mark, which would have been 12:30, Lazarus said: "What do you say we take a break for lunch?"

I must have been so engrossed in the conversation, I didn't acknowledge his request, so about a half hour later he said, "I'm really famished. Let's stop for lunch."

This time, I replied, "I'm just about finished with the interview. Let me ask you a couple of quick wrap-up questions." Again, I bombarded him with a series of questions.

"I am starved. Can we finish this thing while we're having lunch?" he said at what I estimate was around the two o'clock mark.

"I don't do interviews during meals," I commented, "because there is too much interference. But we're almost finished. Just be patient for a few more minutes." Finally at 2:15, I said, "Well, I have no more questions. It's lunchtime!" I received a big "thank you" from a very hungry and appreciative CEO.

The "people are people" lesson was again hammered home to me when I interviewed Muriel Siebert, who, in 1982, was the superintendent of banks of the State of New York, one of the most important regulatory positions in the world of banking. Siebert is also the founder of the securities firm Muriel Siebert & Company, and the first woman ever to own a seat on the New York Stock Exchange. I did my homework well and discovered that my interviewee was nicknamed "Czar Siebert" because she was reputed to run the agency, with a workforce of five hundred plus employees, with an iron hand.

A few minutes before our one o'clock meeting, I arrived at the thirty-second-floor state offices located high above Manhattan's financial district in Two World Trade Tower. It was nearly 1:30 when one of her aides escorted me into her offices. "The superintendent is in one of her mean moods," I was warned as we walked down a long corridor. "Don't be surprised if she gives you only a ten-minute interview. She's been barking at everyone today."

"Thanks for the tip," I replied.

"This is Superintendent Siebert," the aide announced. "Superintendent Siebert, please meet Robert Shook."

"Superintendent Siebert is a long handle, and we don't have a great deal of time to do this interview," I interjected. "Do you mind if I just call you by your nickname, 'Mickie'?" (I had picked up the name from a mutual acquaintance.)

"Er, no, that would be fine," she said, noticeably surprised by my request.

"Now, you can call *me* 'Mr. Shook,' " I said with a straight face. "On second thought, 'Bob' will be just fine," I said with a smile. When she returned my smile it was my tipoff that her reputation as Czar Siebert was not going to be a problem.

About forty-five minutes after the interview began, while she was discussing her youth and having grown up in a competitive environment, I said: "I understand that you once won a Duncan Yo-Yo championship in your hometown, Cleveland." (As always, I had done my homework and had picked up this information in a *Wall Street Journal* article.)

"Yes," she said proudly, "and when the Duncan people read about me in the *Wall Street Journal* article, they sent me a custom-made yo-yo with my picture on it."

"Do you still have it?" I asked.

"Yes. It's in my desk drawer."

"Could I see it?"

"You sure could," she said.

"Gosh, it's a beauty, Mickie. Do you still know how to use it?" When she said yes, I asked her to show me a few tricks.

Siebert proceeded to put on an exhibition that included everything from "rocking the cradle" to "walking the dog."

"So much for the czar image," I thought to myself, as I watched a delightful yo-yo performance.

During my years of selling insurance, I observed that people—from all walks of life—have the same emotions. A rich man reacts the same as a poor man in times of joy, tragedy, anger, frustration—in fact, all emotions. Personal concerns are universal and cross economic boundaries. Each person is concerned about his own health, his sexuality, the aging process, and so on. While wealth provides financial security, it doesn't eliminate emotional insecurities. A man's worth doesn't rule his emotions.

Big Is Better

One aspect about selling to highly successful businesspeople that sets them apart from other people is that they are used

121

to making big decisions. This is one of the contributing factors that makes them successful. So, for good reason, it was early in his career when America's top stockbroker, Martin Shafiroff, made a conscious decision to solicit chairmen, presidents, and treasurers of large companies as well as prominent entrepreneurs throughout the country.

"I am interested in talking to prospects who are at levels whereby they can understand the type of work I do," Shafiroff explains. "I am at my best with people who appreciate sound business ideas. I think that the more knowledgeable they are, the easier it is for me to communicate with them, and accordingly, to create a transaction. It just so happens that these same people have larger net worths than other people, and therefore, when sales occur, they result in large orders.

"I made cold calls to them," he continues, "and talked about my investment strategy. I would say 'From time to time, I come across a company that I strongly believe in, one that is an exceptional business and selling at a significant discount. It represents a tremendous value. When this happens, I would like to chat with you about such an opportunity. Do I have your permission to call you on such an occasion?' When this was agreeable, I sent personal letters to them, again discussing my investment strategy and philosophy. And later, when I would find an exceptional investment that really excited me, I'd call back.

"Most new brokers shy away from these businesspeople, but I decided to go the opposite route," Shafiroff adds. "Now, this does not mean that it is a piece of cake. There are times when it is very difficult to get through to these people. For instance, I just made a large transaction today, but it took me fifteen telephone calls to finally reach the party."

Note that Shafiroff applies the theory of leverage to his successful career. While it might take fifteen calls, the size of the transaction can be more than thirty times the average order of the securities industry.

Today, Shafiroff's total annual transactions run into the billions of dollars. He is believed to have more CEOs of Fortune 500 companies as his clients than any other stockbroker.

Follow the Leader

When I first began lining up interviews to write *The Chief Executive Officers*, I put together a strategy to assure getting the right people to participate in the book. Based on my "follow-the-leader" theory, which had worked for me so well in the insurance field, I chose to go after the biggest CEO first. I contacted General Motors to set up an interview with Thomas Murphy. From my sales experience, I knew that the biggest prospect is recognized as the leader and is not likely to ask: "Who else have you got?" It worked; Murphy never inquired about who else would be in the book. Had Murphy asked, I would have said, "I contacted you first because I knew that once you agreed, the others would be no problem." I thought he would have liked that remark; it always worked in my favor during my sales career.

When the first of the other CEOs asked who was in the book, I'd say, "So far, I have Tom Murphy . . ." and as the list grew, I mentioned more names. By the time I had five or six, the rest were waiting to be asked. In fact, soon the word got out that I was writing the book, and several public relations vice presidents from Fortune 500 companies called to inquire if I would consider their CEOs. They like to follow the leader. Joe Gandolfo refers to the top echelon of prospects in a given industry or community as the good-old-boy club. "These people feel more comfortable when their peers have signed up too," he explains.

As I mentioned earlier, most people have a difficult time making decisions that are out of their area of expertise. Consequently, they feel more comfortable when they know others whom they respect have also made the same decision. Of course, just to mention the name of any prospect is not necessarily a convincing reason to go along with the group. An individual who isn't respected for making wise decisions might even work against you. You must choose carefully those people whom you want to serve as leaders. You must drop names with discretion. And if you don't have an impressive clientele or major individual, just reply: "I am sorry, but I am not at liberty to tell you at this time."

The Dangers of a Small Order

Sometimes a buyer will "test the waters" with a small initial order, and, with good service, eventually increase it. As the saying goes, "from little acorns grow mighty oaks." This is so obvious that it's not necessary to elaborate on this subject. What is worthy of discussion, however, is how a small order can possibly be worse than no order whatsoever.

Note, for example, a sales representative for the Bedtime Mattress Company with a territory covering the state of Indiana. There are three potential retailers in Muncie, a city with an approximate population of seventy thousand, and Bedtime seeks one store to be its exclusive dealer. The sales rep calls on Peter Babbitt, the owner of Babbitt's, a fine furniture store, who agrees to carry the Bedtime line in addition to the three other brands of mattresses that the store sells. However, he will only place an initial order of four units. The salesman realizes that by selling to Babbitt's, his line will be a secondary source. However, it is possible that two other Muncie retailers are potential accounts that will carry the Bedtime line as their primary mattress source. Under these circumstances, it may be unwise to permit Babbitt's to carry the line in spite of being the area's leading furniture store. To do so would severely limit Bedtime's sales in Muncie.

Another danger of a small order is that the retailer would pay little attention to its promotion of a secondary line. As a result, the inventory would not turn over, thereby hampering future reordering. It is not in your best interest to have a buyer think of you as a small-potato salesperson—and consequently, only toss you a few crumbs now and then, saving the big orders for his big-potato resource.

Likewise, Dean Wittman, a stockbroker, might receive a token order, one hundred shares of a stock trading at fifteen dollars. Even though he considers the sale as a door opener for future business, the client uses two other security representatives for his major investments. By opening several new accounts each week with minute orders, Wittman is lulled into a feeling of false security. It isn't the number of accounts a salesperson has on the books that puts money into his bank account; it's the size of his commission checks. This does not suggest that small orders are not worthwhile, but is rather a recommendation to be aware that the only test of success in selling is measured by your bottom line.

Don't Assume Too Much

While hardball selling advocates assuming you will close every sale, there is one thing you must *avoid* assuming: Do not assume that the biggest and best prospects in your territory have already been sold by somebody else.

This is a lesson I learned a long time ago—before I entered the sales field. When I was in college, I was shy about asking the best-looking girls on campus for dates. I *assumed* that the most beautiful ones were booked up for weeks at a time. "Besides," I thought, "why would they want to date me when they could have any guy they wanted?" Luckily, when a fraternity brother offered to fix me up on a blind date with his sister, I accidentally discovered that the beauties were available after all. "Do me a favor, will you, Bob, and take Linda to the homecoming dance," Stan asked. "She doesn't have much of a social life and I'd like for her to meet some of the guys."

As it turned out, Linda was beautiful and absolutely delightful. In fact, my date with her was a major highlight of my college career. Surprisingly, Linda told me that she rarely dated. It was obviously because all the guys assumed she was unavailable and were afraid to ask her out. Never again did I hesitate to call other "unapproachable women." I ascertained that there was less competition to date the most desirable coeds on campus because other guys were gun-shy about approaching them.

Later, I applied what I had learned about unapproachable women to my sales career. Although I observed other salespeople who were apprehensive about calling on highly successful prospects, I never hesitated. "He's a big wheel," they'd say, or "He owns that huge company." Consequently, they would stay away from the prospects who appeared unapproachable. Actually, because the best prospects were not inundated by hordes of salespeople, they were actually easier to sell. As a bonus, when dealing with the "big wheels," there are no turndowns resulting from a lack of money.

Joe Gandolfo points out: "When I call on somebody with the money to buy my product, I assume that because he's given me an interview, I am going to sell him. The guy must be interested or he wouldn't agree to talk to me about insurance. So, it is not a matter of 'Can he afford it?' but rather, 'How much will he spend?' "

The 80 Percent/20 Percent Rule

More often than not, 80 percent of a salesperson's sales volume comes from 20 percent of his accounts. Of course, depending on what you sell, the numbers vary, but a review of your customers is likely to support the fact that you should concentrate on your bigger accounts and spend less time on smaller ones.

This advice shouldn't be construed to mean that you should blatantly neglect accounts that generate meager commissions. Small customers can become big customers. Rather than neglecting anyone, you must regularly evaluate your customers and determine who deserves the most attention. After all, there are only so many hours in each day in which to be productive, and you don't want to spread yourself too thin at the expense of your prime accounts.

There are theories that advocate treating all customers with equality, claiming that it is sacrilegious to do otherwise. Then too, every so often a large corporation's spokesperson is heard from atop a soapbox: "We value every customer equally, irrespective of his or her size. Each of our customers receives identical service." Rubbish! In the real world, key accounts that provide larger profits are acknowledged as more valuable than small, marginal ones. Common sense dictates it is poor business for a salesperson to exert the same amount of time and effort with customers that predictably generate $50 commissions versus others, say, in the $10,000 commission range. This is poor time management and worse, it's bad business.

Once again, you are reminded to concentrate on bigger prospects, which, when orders are placed, compensate you with substantially larger commission checks. In the real estate field, for example, two brokers working on a 6 percent commission rate will realize vastly different earnings when one sells a property valued at $50,000 and the other for $1 million. The salesperson who specializes in the $50,000 range must make twenty sales to earn the same amount of commissions as his counterpart. While it is true that there are fewer prospects in the market for the more expensive property, the time and effort required to make this sale is certainly not twenty times greater. Likewise, a $2 million life insurance policy is not forty times more difficult to sell than a $50,000 policy. In actuality, selling to the well-to-do is often effortless in comparison to addressing the cash-poor buyer.

A sales representative selling merchandise to a large retailer such as K Mart or Wal-Mart can generate commissions that exceed those of the combined orders from a thousand mom-and-pop accounts. Furthermore, it is likely that a certain percentage of the small retailers has poor credit ratings that will nullify what were hard-earned commission checks. This is not a factor you need to consider if your account has a triple A credit rating.

Every so often a salesperson will shy away from going after the giant accounts on the grounds that it is poor business to put all your eggs in one basket. This same individual will say: "By not having large accounts, I won't get hurt when I lose any single small account." This is nonsensical and a weak excuse for shying away from large accounts. In fact, I strongly suspect people who think in this manner are simply afraid of their own inadequacies as salespersons. Of course, when you do put a large number of your eggs in one basket, I advise you to watch that basket very carefully!

The statistics being what they are, a hardball salesperson must always have a keen awareness of the 80/20 rule. This doesn't imply, however, that you should skip over small customers altogether. Instead, you must pick and choose which small accounts have potential to grow into large accounts. As a general rule, a mom-and-pop business operated by the same individual(s) for many years is unlikely to be transformed into a major concern. But you may want to "grow" with a new start-up business that has a unique concept, particularly if you believe its founders are bright and aggressive. The Wasserstrom Co., a regional restaurant equipment and supplies company in Columbus, Ohio, for instance, sold to Wendy's when the international fast-food franchiser opened its first store in 1969. Wasserstrom management had confidence in Wendy's founder David Thomas, a hard-working, ambitious man who had previous fast-food experience. The company was willing to "carry" Thomas for a short period when the business was in its infancy, and today, with more than 3,700 outlets, Wendy's is unquestionably the largest Wasserstrom account.

Similarly, when Ray Kroc, at age fifty-two, acquired the original McDonald brothers' hamburger store in San Bernardino, California, in 1954, even Kroc himself couldn't have imagined that there would someday be more than eleven thousand Golden Arches outlets. The original suppliers of products, ranging from paper cups to hamburger patty wrappers, could not have anticipated the phenomenal account that McDonald's represented. Study the names of companies that appear on the Fortune 500 list and note the surprisingly large number of organizations that weren't in business a quarter of a century ago!

Growing with the right new business can be immensely profitable. Top life insurance agents have clients who initially apply for $10,000 policies and later purchase $1 million policies. Real estate brokers who sell small "starter" homes to young couples have later sold properties to the same buyers with price tags and commission checks twenty times as high. And many stockbrokers have opened small accounts with first-time orders totaling a few thousand dollars that eventually ran into seven figures.

How do you determine *which* small customers have the potential that warrant being nurtured and with whom you can grow? First you should periodically review your accounts and weed out those that are stagnant. Look for patterns that include such things as infrequent orders or small orders from those who are habitually late in paying. An objective review will quickly disclose which customers are weak and therefore should be given a minimum amount of time and effort to develop. In some fields, such as insurance, securities, and real estate, common sense will dictate which clients represent potential growth. For instance, a stockbroker might get initial orders in the amount of $10,000 from both a young executive with General Motors and an assembly line worker, each having annual incomes in the $25,000 range. It's a good assumption, however, that the young executive's future earning power will be substantially greater ten years down the road than the blue collar worker's. Likewise, while both may buy a $50,000 life insurance policy, the young executive is the better candidate for larger future purchases.

After carefully analyzing your customer base, there should be no problem identifying those with excellent potential growth. These are the ones you should concentrate on nurturing. Of course, there may be a handful of borderline customers who are more difficult to size up. When this happens, take your time. There is no urgency to drop these dubious ones. Whenever you are uncertain, give them the benefit of the doubt. After all, it's easier to drop a customer than to find a new one.

Turning Little Orders into Big Orders

Once the sale is secured, it's a good percentage play to go for a bigger sale. For example, after a prospect agrees to buy a $500,000 life insurance policy, the agent might suggest that the amount really necessary to adequately cover the prospect's needs is $1 million. Once the prospect is committed to buy, it takes little additional effort to ask for a larger order. In comparison to the enormous amount of work required to seek out a new prospect and make another $500,000 sale, this simple, effective suggestion is effortless. The upside represents a sizable return in relation to the minimal downside risk of losing the initial sale by making the suggestion to buy additional insurance. Understanding risk/return ratios enables a salesperson to generate considerable extra commissions during a year's time.

Ed Ellman, a leading life insurance agent in Columbus, Ohio, frequently requests that an insurer issue two policies when, in fact, the applicant has only applied for one. "Let's say a client applies for one-million-dollar policy," Ellman explains. "Well, two one-million policies are issued, and I deliver both of them to the client. 'Congratulations. You passed your examination! In fact you did so well, I took the liberty of having the underwriting department insure you for twice the original amount. I determined that as long as you're currently enjoying excellent health, you would want to take advantage of getting the second policy. You are under no obligation to take it, but if you want my recommendation. I think you should have it.'

"I do this with clients whom I believe need more than the amount they applied for," Ellman continues. "It takes practically no effort whatsoever to do this and when I do get an extra sale, it can mean a substantial commission. I pick up a few extra sales each year with this technique, and with a big policy the added commissions range between ten thousand and twenty thousand dollars. I don't think there is a downside risk because I have never lost the original sale by attempting to make an extra one. In fact, when somebody does not go for the second policy, he will usually apologize by saying something like. 'I appreciate your concern, Ed, but I'm going to pass. Thanks anyhow.' "

Ellman is an excellent percentage player; the minimal effort he exerts by bringing along a second policy rewards him with hefty commission checks. To put it another way, he adds: "If I were to calculate my hourly wage for effort put into selling the second policy, it would be many times the rate of the first policy, which included effort spent prospecting, setting up the initial appointment, creating the need, and so on."

Another insurance agent sells additional options upon having a buyer commit to buying a basic policy. The agent sells features ranging from the waiver of premium to double indemnity. Some salespeople hike the price (and their commission checks) of automobiles by selling optional equipment such as a sunroof, cruise control, metallic paint, and undercoating. Likewise, a copy machine salesperson sells extras over and above the basic equipment, options that do everything from increasing and decreasing the size of the copy to collating and stapling.

Just how this works is well illustrated in Stanley Marcus's book *Quest for the Best*. Marcus describes how Dean Ferguson, a young buyer in the Neiman-Marcus men's clothing department, turned a fifteen-dollar necktie purchase into a major sale.

> [He asked her] "What is he going to wear it with?" The woman reached into her purse and pulled out a swatch of fabric. Dean looked at it for a moment, and said, "There's an ancient madder pattern which comes in two color combinations that would go very well with this suit." He pulled out the two ties as he was talking to her. She readily agreed and took both of them—at $22.50 each.

Dean asked, "Doesn't he need some new shirts to go with his new suit?" The customer replied, "I'm so glad you asked; he does need some, but I haven't been able to find any white ones with French cuffs. Do you have any size fifteen–thirty-three?" He showed her two qualities, pointing out the difference in the cloths. She selected three of the more expensive shirts at $40 each. "Doesn't he ever wear colored shirts?" Dean inquired. 'Yes, and if you have this same shirt in blue I'll take two.' "

The woman's buying spree also included a pair of cuff links for $50, a $165 travel robe with a matching ascot, two pairs of $45 pajamas, and a pair of $50 Italian soft calf lounging slippers. He points out that "a sale of $615 which was built on the $15 tie [resulted in] an increase of 4000 percent. What was of even more importance, he had made a firm new customer for the department." As you can see, the large increased sale was not viewed as high pressure; to Stanley Marcus, one of the world's great retailers, it was a matter of giving outstanding service.

Selling more than what a buyer thinks he is initially in the market to buy is often in the customer's best interest. This is especially true when a prospect doesn't know enough about what he wants, or has no familiarity with current market prices. Pat Howland, a leading real estate agent who sells homes in the half-million- to one-million-dollar range in Bexley, Ohio, explains how she often shows properties priced higher than what prospects had originally planned to spend. "An out-of-town buyer who is transferred to Columbus may not be familiar with the cost of homes in our market," she points out. "For example, a couple may tell me they are looking for a home in the $500,000 range, and for this amount of money, they want five bedrooms, a large lot, central air conditioning and so on. After I am certain they can afford to spend more to find their dream house, I will show them homes in the $600,000 to $700,000 range.

"Of course, I'll tell them in advance," Howland continues, " 'now I know this is more than you planned to spend, but there is nothing on the market for $500,000 that will provide you with what you're looking for. I'd like to show you a home with an asking price of $625,000, but keep in mind that it has been totally remodeled with a new kitchen, new central air conditioning, and a new master bathroom. It was just beautifully decorated, and I know you will love what they've done. You could move today and not have to do a thing to it. As you know from the homes I've already showed you in this neighborhood, these stately old homes require a lot of work. So when you consider what has to be done to refurbish them, this one is a real bargain if you can afford the higher price.' " Howland emphasizes that she does not purposely try to oversell anyone, "but it is sometimes necessary to show more expensive properties so that a couple will be happy in their new home. Otherwise, it is only a matter of time before they regret having bought it."

Think Big!

It is sometimes easier to sell something big to somebody big than to sell something small to somebody small. By now, you must certainly be aware that a constant theme throughout this book is to *think big*. New York billionaire Harry Helmsley, one of America's most successful real estate developers, stresses: "There is really not a great deal of difference between the 'big ones' and the 'little ones.' " And when asked to compare a large real estate transaction to a small one, he says, "It's the same deal, except you just add another naught here and there. Actually, it's really easier to make a $6.5

million deal than a $65,000 deal. It's just a question of how many naughts you have. The principles are the same."

One of the most successful real estate brokers I ever met was Rich Port, who operated an enormous residential sales organization with twenty-eight offices in Greater Chicago. Port told me that when he decided to enter the sales field, he only considered selling something that was big. Nothing is physically larger than real estate. Like Rich Port, hardball selling advocates selling something big, but physical size is not always a prerequisite. A product's price tag is the prime consideration whether you're selling diamonds, computer systems, life insurance, securities, heavy equipment, or, for that matter, paper products to McDonald's. Furthermore, it is not necessarily the cost of each unit, especially when you sell in large volumes. And, of course, the bottom line is the size of your paycheck. With this in mind, you should also consider the commission schedule because, while some products are sold in large dollar volumes, they don't always generate high commissions. Obviously, a salesperson's earning capacity is limited when he is compensated mostly by salary rather than straight commission. In our free enterprise system, a hardball salesperson is willing to assume the risks of a commission sales career because he thinks big and believes in his selling skills.

In order to sell a billion dollars' worth of life insurance in a single year, like Joe Gandolfo, a salesperson must think big. Just how did Gandolfo do it? "A salesperson has to believe in his product one hundred percent," he says. "Do you know that before I owned a million-dollar policy on my own life, I had a difficult time selling one to anyone else? Then, when I owned one, it became easy for me to talk to somebody else about having that much life insurance. The same thing was true with selling tax shelters. Once I began putting my money into tax shelters, I had no problem convincing other people to put their money into them because I believed in the product. There is something about somebody asking, 'Say, Joe, are you in it?' and being able to respond, 'Yeah, I've got my money in it, too.' That conviction does wonders for persuading the other guy."

A common notion about the money made in selling is that "the sky is the limit." That depends upon what you sell; salespeople with equal selling skills aren't as a matter of course equally compensated. For instance, Nancy and Lois both sell residential real estate, but Nancy sells homes in an affluent neighborhood in the $500,000 to $2 million range. Lois sells homes in a middle-income neighborhood, with price tags ranging from $75,000 to $150,000. Both work on a gross commission of 5 percent. In May, Nancy sold two homes at $800,000 and $900,000. She earned $85,000 in commissions. Los sold four homes for $85,000, $115,000, $190,000, and $210,000. It was her biggest month ever, and her commissions totaled $30,000. To excel as a hardball salesperson you must always think big and go for the big sales. After all, if you build a block of business consisting of small accounts with no potential for growth, you will always have a block of business consisting of small accounts. Doing this is a sure way to make selling unnecessarily time-consuming and difficult, which is not particularly smart or economical. As a hardball salesperson, you will instinctively think big—and make big commission checks!

7

Creating a Sense of Urgency

The four principles of hardball selling impart how and why people frequently delay making buying decisions even though they should buy. One sure way to light a fire under procrastinators is by creating a sense of urgency. To do this, you must give them a strong reason why they will benefit by acting immediately. This is accomplished by convincing them that they have something to gain by making an immediate decision—or to lose if they do not.

It should be noted that, while most prospects need an incentive to be motivated to make on-the-spot buying decisions, this is not true with all people. In some instances, prospects are presold before a sales presentation, and only a routine demonstration or explanation of the product is necessary to make the sale. The trouble is that these "sure sales" are so infrequent that they do not provide a salesperson with an adequate income. As the saying goes, "Even a blind pig will stumble across some corn." But don't count on it.

A hardball salesperson gets his share of these easy sales, which he naturally accepts. However, it is the difficult ones he also gets that make him stand out from the crowd. Often he closes these sales by making the prospect feel an urgent need to buy now—*before it is too late.*

"Too late for what?" you might ask. *Too late* means that the set of circumstances for buying will not be the same later as it is today. The hardball salesperson stresses that something will be different from what it is now, and this change may have some adverse effect on the buyer. By creating this scenario, the buyer encounters a negative option that can be avoided by making an immediate buying decision.

A Sense of Timing

Many businesspeople live by the creed that "timing is everything." In some businesses, this is a given. A stockbroker, in particular, creates a sense of urgency by making his client aware of how timing affects a stock purchase. "As you know," he says, "with important business decisions, timing is everything. With General Engines priced at eighty, I feel that this is the right time to buy. We are looking at a low multiple of only six, which is considerably lower than the industry's. And based on a current yield of seven percent coupled with this morning's announcement of the third quarter's earnings, we should place an order of five thousand shares." Here, the appeal is made to the buyer's greed. The message is "The longer the delay, the more it will cost."

This "timing is everything" tactic can be used to sell practically any product. A car salesman says: "We're anticipating a price increase any day now. Every time the phone rings, my sales manager thinks it's the call for the higher sticker prices." A clothing manufacturer's rep says: "We have had six price increases from the mill this year, and another one is due any day now. Let's put your order in immediately so we can guarantee this price to you."

A travel agent uses the same strategy to get a commitment

from his client. "I will book you today so we can guarantee you this fare. The way tickets keep going up, this fare may not be available tomorrow."

In the above examples, the timing factor is based on price increases; however, it could also be based on availability of the product, solutions to present costly problems, or a personal characteristic, such as age, of a specific prospect.

Finding Solutions

With many products, closing the sale is contingent on finding a solution to a prospect's problem. This is especially true when selling such things as advertising, computers, consulting services, copying machines, and high-tech products. Once a salesperson demonstrates how his product will solve a pressing problem, the customer feels an urgent need to implement the solution. The longer the delay, the more the problem continues to impede the customer. It often costs money *to do nothing*. Problems generally do not go away by themselves.

Sometimes a salesperson must create an immediate sense of urgency during his initial approach. Jay Bernstein calls it his "gangbusters approach":

In 1965, when I was just beginning to pick up major stars, I used this approach with Robert Culp, who, at the time, was starring with Bill Cosby in the television series *I Spy*. Although Culp didn't know me from Adam, I burst into his dressing room unannounced and said in my most authoritative voice, "Culp, the name is Jay Bernstein with Jay Bernstein Public Relations. You better sit down and listen to what I have to say. *Your career is in big trouble!*"

Culp was standing there in between sets in his underwear getting ready to change clothes. He had a stunned expression on his face and was speechless.

I pointed to the only chair in the room and he sat down.
"Trouble? What kind of trouble?"

"Is Cosby around?" I asked in a hushed voice.

"We share this dressing room," he replied. "But no, he's not here now."

"Good," I said, "because as you know, there have been some rumors going around that the two of you are not getting along. And the way the public is hearing it, they're siding with Cosby, not you."

"It's nothing serious," Culp replied. "Is it?"

"Culp, if things continue on their present course, it wouldn't surprise me if your career goes under."

"It looks that bad?"

"Yes, smack down the tubes. But I can turn it around for you," I said in a reassuring manner.

"It so happens I've been thinking about looking into hiring somebody to handle my PR," he said, and stuck out his hand to shake mine. "I like your style, Bernstein. I need somebody with your kind of chutzpah."

I signed him up for a thousand dollars a month, and we've been close friends ever since.

Emanuel Temple, an advertising specialty rep, opened a large account with a Big Three company by using a similar approach:

It was only a matter of seconds after being ushered into the buyer's office when I said, "Do you know what I consider the most important component in a car?"

"No. What?" the buyer asked.

"It's the owner's manual. Because the company is required to put one in every car. Without it, the customer doesn't know how to operate his car properly and will have all kinds of problems."

Having said this, I took out a salami sandwich wrapped in cellophane and placed it on the table. "Your owner's manual is packaged like a salami sandwich!"

Temple got the buyer's attention by creating a sense of urgency—he demonstrated that a change was in order. Today, he sells millions of owner's manual portfolios to the automobile manufacturer.

My eighteen-year-old son, Michael, and I recently drove out to Honda East in Michael's dilapidated junker and met with Bert Lindsay, the dealership's owner. After looking at several models, Michael had his eye on a Prelude. However, since I was the one who was going to write the check, I said, "We'll come back in a day or two, Bert . . . if we decide to buy it."

Lindsay was not about to let us walk so easily. "As long as you're here, Bob, do you mind if I take a look at Michael's car?" he asked. "I'll give you a quote on a trade-in."

"Great," Michael said, "I'm parked in front."

After looking over the car, Lindsay said, "Good heavens! Look at those tires, Bob. They are so bald, the rubber is worn down to the steel belts."

"Yeah, I was a nervous wreck driving out here on the freeway," I said, glaring at my son.

"Bob, there is no way I'm going to let you drive home in this junker," Lindsay said. "If you don't buy a car today, I insist that you drive a loaner. I don't want you getting killed on I-70 on your way out of here."

Lindsay knew I would not feel comfortable imposing on his generosity. He also knew that he had backed me into a corner and was forcing me to make a quick decision. And he knew that Michael was on his side.

My son drove me home in his new Honda Prelude that night.

When it comes to selling products that are used in business, a sense of urgency is created by emphasizing that the buyer is losing money when his buying decision is delayed. With a computer system, for example, a salesperson stresses: "Every day you put off installing this system, the antiquated bookkeeping procedure that handles your payroll is costing you money." A heavy equipment salesperson states: "This machinery will pay for itself in two years with the money it saves in labor." A word processor sales representative explains: "Your secretary's efficiency and output will increase threefold." When the case is properly presented, businesspeople feel they can not afford to delay decisions that solve their problems.

Lack of Availability

Creating a sense of urgency by presenting a lack of availability ranges from the common limited-offer technique to the highest levels of negotiations. As its name implies, the limited offer is a simple, direct attempt to close a sale by restricting certain terms of the sale to a definite time frame upon which the offer expires. Such offers might be a two-day sale by a local retailer, a discount coupon that is good only through the fifteenth of the month, or a manufacturer's rebate if the product is purchased within thirty days of the offer.

Richard Larimer, a Xerox marketing representative who sold me my copier, closed the sale with a limited offer. Later, he told me that he used this technique because I already owned a ten-year-old Xerox, which was working well but did not have the capacity of the newer machine.

After Larimer gave a demonstration, I commented: "It really has some excellent features that are superior to ours. But there's no rush to make an immediate decision since ours is adequate. I'll call you in a few days and let you know what we'll do."

"Do you realize that the service agreement on your present machine costs as much as the monthly payments on a new machine?" Larimer said.

"But with the new machine, I'll have to pay a service charge too, won't I?"

"For the first three years, there isn't any," he explained. "And until the end of the month, which, incidentally, is tomorrow, we have a special that includes four years of free service. And, until the end of the month, we're offering zero percent financing."

"Let's go over the exact numbers," I said with renewed interest.

During an interview with Larimer to find out more about Xerox's selling techniques, he discussed those which create a sense of urgency. Larimer told me: "We generally have some kind of a limited offer that runs for a month to three months. It can be free service for a given period of time, promotional interest rates, cash discounts, free supplies, or perhaps a bonus gift, such as a small copier or typewriter. In each instance, it is an incentive to motivate the customer to make a buying decision."

Of course, with a one-of-a-kind product, a built-in sense of urgency exists because if the buyer procrastinates, another buyer might purchase the product. The purchase of my home is a good example. My wife and I drove by it on a daily basis while it was being constructed. It had been on the market for about six months when I received a visit from my friend Whit Dillon, a local realtor.

"Bob, I want to set up an appointment with you and Bobbie to see your new house," Whit said.

"Our new house?" I asked.

"Yeah, the one on South Drexel Avenue," he replied.

Dillon showed us the house, and it was obvious that we liked it.

"But we have to discuss it between ourselves, Whit. I'm sure you understand," I said.

"Of course," he replied. "Mary and I are the same way. But I must point out that this is not my listing and there are three other brokers showing it later today and tomorrow morning."

He then quoted us the price and added, "They reduced their asking price by fifty grand, and at this figure it will be sold by noon tomorrow."

"Come on," I said, "you're talking to me, Whit. This house has been on the market for six months."

"Yeah, I know, Bob. But not at this price. I'm telling you that if you don't put in a bid today, somebody else will."

"Bob, could we talk in private?" my wife nudged me. With that we excused ourselves and she dragged me into the den.

"How are you two doing in there?" Whit asked from the hallway a few minutes later.

"We just finished our little chat," Bobbie answered. She gave me a big hug as we walked out of the room.

"I need both of you to sign these papers," he said with a chuckle.

"You son of a gun," I muttered. "You know damn well nobody's going to make an offer in the next twenty-four hours."

For the record, we signed the papers on the spot and we lived in the house for seventeen wonderful years. When I finally sold it, its value had increased more than fourfold. While I *still* believe Whit applied high pressure by creating a sense of urgency, I have always been grateful that he did.

I suppose it was poetic justice that Whit used a close on me that I, too, have used many times. In fact, to convince one of my insurance agents that creating a sense of urgency is effective, I once devised a lead card with a large "Eligibility" number stamped on it. This small index card was filled with computer holes, and it contained a few facts about a prospect such as his name, address, and occupation. Armed with these cards, the agent and I spent an entire day making calls on small business owners.

One particular prospect told me that he liked the policy but would not make a decision until he had slept on it. "I understand how you feel," I replied. Then as I wrote on the card, I repeated the words: "To Whom It May Concern: Robert Shook has explained to me the coverage for which I am eligible to apply. I understand that the above eligibility number on this card will expire as of midnight. I further understand that he will not call on me in the future."

I handed the card to the prospect and said, "Would you please sign and date this for me?"

He studied it carefully and said, "I'm not going to sign that."

"I would appreciate it if you would, sir, so our records indicate that I was here and you decided to relinquish your number," I explained with an air of authority.

"What is the least amount I could apply for and not lose my number?" he asked. "And if I take out a small plan now, can I increase it to a more expensive plan later?"

"As long as your health does not change, you can up it to a higher one later."

When we left his place of business, my agent laughingly said, "He didn't buy insurance, Bob. He bought a number from you. I didn't realize we were in the numbers business!"

A sense of urgency can be created for practically any type of product when you limit its availability to the buyer. This technique even works when no *real* need exists to make a buying decision, such as with a luxury item. For instance, Diana Bloch, a successful travel agent in Columbus, Ohio, tells a client when selling a once-in-a-lifetime, around-the-world trip on a luxury cruise liner: "What are you waiting for? This is a trip that you have been wanting and saving for all of your lives. If you put it off now, the chances are you'll never go. I know you probably feel guilty about treating yourselves to such an expensive vacation, but you deserve it. After all, after years of hard work, isn't this what it's really all about?" Following a slight pause to allow the thought to sink in, she adds, "Now, this particular trip is filling up fast and there are only a few choice cabins left from which to choose." Then Bloch closes the sale by asking, "Which of these two air-sea packages shall I reserve for you?"

Bloch points out that she is effective with this close because she makes her clients realize that they are denying themselves luxuries to which they are entitled after many hard years of work. She proceeds to create an urgency to act immediately by emphasizing that there are only a few openings, and they may not be available if the decision-making is delayed. So, even at $40,000 to $50,000 per person, the prospects feel an urgent need to sign up now.

Setting the Stage

To avoid procrastination and create urgency you must set the stage for decisiveness. Imagine, for example, a high-powered, executive-type salesperson delivering a flawless sales presentation, full of facts, covering every aspect of why it is essential to make an immediate buying decision. The salesperson's integrity and professionalism generate complete confidence. What's more, it is in the client's best interest to place an immediate order, and the client feels it. Under this scenario, it is probable that the prospect will avoid disappointing this salesman by requesting time to think matters over; instead he or she will feel obligated to take decisive action.

Creating a buying atmosphere of this nature generally begins during or even before your initial contact with a prospect. It may start with your reputation in the business community as a hard-charging, no-nonsense person. Or you may portray a VIP image as a result of letters and brochures mailed to the prospect prior to your first meeting. It is a matter of setting the stage in a manner that you believe promotes you as a results-driven individual. The more the prospect sees you in this light, the less likely he is to vacillate when the sale is closed.

Joe Gandolfo knows this well and pulls no punches when he makes an appointment to sell life insurance to an out-of-town prospect. He explains: "I don't want to travel to some faraway city and at the end of the presentation be told, 'It sounds great, but I have to talk it over with my controller (attorney, partner, etc.).' So after I have set up an appointment, I cover myself by saying, 'I want you to be certain to include at our meeting anyone whose presence you believe is necessary in order for a decision to be made at that time. Now, I don't care who is there, your attorney, CPA, controller, partner, whoever. I'll be happy to answer any questions any of them may have.' "

By saying this in the beginning. Gandolfo eliminates the possibility of a prospect offering a lame excuse at the close of the presentation. "When a prospect says he is the decision-maker." Gandolfo continues, "I congratulate him by saying: 'It is good to meet a person who is capable of making a decision on his own without a committee.' This comment puts pressure on him to be decisive because, if he procrastinates, he is going against his word. Of course, if it is not possible for him alone to make a buying decision, I don't want to waste my time giving him alone a sales presentation. Then the prospect will include one or more persons whose presence is necessary for a decision to be made to sit in on the interview. When there are two or more partners, it is particularly important to have everyone present; certain purchases may otherwise be in violation of the partnership agreement."

For the same reason, a real estate broker might insist on having both husband and wife available to view a house. A decision to purchase a home is generally jointly made because it is a major, long-term investment. Then too, other factors are involved ranging from interior decorating to financing that require both spouses to be present.

Of course, depending upon the product, it may not be necessary to have both husband and wife there. Obviously, minor purchases rarely require both to share in the decision-making. With some products such as life insurance, automobiles, and investments, it could go either way. What you do want to avoid is a situation whereby, at the end of your sales presentation, somebody says: "I like it, but I could never do anything about it without first discussing it with my wife." To avoid this, you must be up-front and ask if it is necessary for the spouse to be present. When told that this is not necessary, reply: "It is a pleasure to meet somebody like yourself who is capable of making his own decision. You would be surprised how many people are unable to make up their minds." Often this remark is taken as a challenge—the prospect does not want to look foolish by procrastinating after he has been complimented on his independence.

Another direct question to consider asking a prospect before getting into the actual sales presentation might be: "Do you have the authority to make a five-thousand-dollar decision?" Again, when somebody says that he does, it is embarrassing to later say that he does not.

When you make it clear prior to the actual sales presentation that you expect a decision to be made immediately, the prospect feels pressured to act on the spot. After all, you have clearly told him that this is what you expect him to do. By your setting the stage in this manner, an aura of urgency prevails that works in your favor during the close of the sale.

Let the Buyer Sell You

A successful business transaction must benefit the seller and the buyer. Accordingly, both parties must feel satisfied or a poor deal has transpired. This translates to mean that you, the seller, must also be sold on having the buyer as your customer: If getting an order is bad business for you, then you don't want it. When you can relay the message that, under certain circumstances, you would walk away without a sale, the buyer is placed in a position where he must do some selling to convince you to do business with him. The more he sells, the more there is a sense of urgency to complete an immediate deal. This is sometimes referred to as "reverse selling" due to the element of reverse psychology that makes people want what they can't easily obtain. It works best by first creating the need, and then making it hard to fulfill!

I used this technique when my book, *The Perfect Sales Presentation*, was sold to Bantam Books. When my agent, Al Zuckerman, told me that Bantam was interested in my proposal, I asked him to set up a twenty-minute meeting for me with the editor in chief and a senior editor. The following week, I flew into New York to see them.

At the start of the meeting, I placed my watch on the conference table and said: "My reasons for wanting to meet with you personally are twofold: First, since this is a book about selling, I want you to witness firsthand that I am an expert on the subject. If I cannot sell you on *The Perfect Sales Presentation*, then you should clearly not consider buying it. Secondly, I believe that it is vital for a publishing house to share the author's enthusiasm for his work, especially on a book of this nature. So, I will carefully observe your reactions while I make my presentation. If you are not consumed with enthusiasm when our twenty-minute conversation has expired, then you are not the right publisher for this book."

For the remaining twenty minutes, I stressed why my book was completely different from any other publication. Most important, I discussed why so many salespeople would want to read it, and I pointed out several ways in which Bantam could reach those markets. When I finished, I put my watch back on my wrist, and while doing so, out of the corner of my eye, I observed the editor in chief and editor glancing at one another. Each gave a slight nod of approval to the other. I waited during a few moments of silence.

"We'd like to publish your book, Bob," the editor in chief said.

"You don't seem overwhelmed with enthusiasm," I commented.

"What do you want us to do?" the editor retorted. "Jump up and down on the conference table? We are completely sold," she emphasized.

"I would like to hear about Bantam's distribution system, and what you plan to do to promote my book."

For the next fifteen minutes, they both discussed how Bantam had one of the premier marketing organizations in the publishing industry (which I already knew), and each presented her ideas on potential ways to hype *The Perfect Sales Presentation.*

The editor in chief repeated, "We want to publish your book."

After a few seconds of silence, I said, "I would like for you to do that too. I suggest that you contact Al Zuckerman at Writers House. Since he is my agent, I do not think it is appropriate for me to discuss any of the terms of the agreement directly with you."

"Thank you for letting us have an opportunity to discuss your manuscript with you," the editor said.

"I will be meeting with two other publishers this afternoon," I continued. "I recommend that you contact Zuckerman as soon as possible." By adding this, I created a sense of urgency that communicated: "You'd better act now before you lose this book to another publisher."

"We will contact him this afternoon and make an offer," the editor in chief answered.

In an industry where writers go begging to have their work published, I let Bantam sell me on why they should be my publisher. Then too, a bidding situation was created as a result of my having a one-of-a-kind product. When this occurs, a buyer must act quickly, or endure an unwanted consequence, which, in Bantam's case, was losing the manuscript to another publisher. I did with Bantam what Whit Dillon did with me when I purchased a house from him. Obviously, under the right set of circumstances, this technique works quite well.

A manufacturer's rep can do it when he sells his line to a single dealer in a specific territory. By offering exclusivity, retailers must compete to "earn the right to carry the line." The rep says: "I am not convinced that you are the right company to represent us in this area. Tell me why you deserve the opportunity to prove yourself to my firm. Give me some ammunition I can use to sell my sales manager on you." A nice touch of subtlety is added when he says, "I'm in your corner, and I would personally like to see you be chosen as our account. Now what could I say to present a strong case on your behalf?"

Likewise, an insurance agent informs a prospect that he must qualify for the policy by passing certain health requirements. "Your family health history and past high blood pressure readings raise some doubt that this application will be accepted," the agent says.

"My blood pressure only shot up during a stressful period

when I was going through some difficult times with my work," the prospect interjects.

"Unfortunately, it is on your permanent health record. I will mention that in my report. I will do my best for you, but I can't make you any promises," the agent explains. Similarly, a computer salesperson might generate the same reaction from a prospect by emphasizing the difficulty in obtaining credit so that a costly system may be installed. Or a real estate broker points out that a young couple's combined incomes may not be high enough to qualify for financing. In each instance, when reverse selling of this nature is properly executed, the prospect's thinking focuses more on qualifying than on delaying the buying decision.

Having a No-Callback Policy Creates Urgency

Oftentimes, being up-front with people is the best way to overcome procrastination and simultaneously create a sense of urgency. I have already explained that hardball salespeople do not make callbacks. Ever. When a prospect requests that you come back in a few days for his decision, tell him: "I'm sorry, but I don't make callbacks." Procrastination is then impossible.

Following this, you can explain: "I have just reviewed all of the information about why you should buy, and you should make your decision now while everything is fresh in your mind. I recognize that you are a busy person and have a lot of things going on in your life. By tomorrow, in all probability, you will not retain everything that I have explained to you. And, as each day passes, you will be less able to make a buying decision. If I let you procrastinate, I would be negligent in my job and doing you a disservice. I am too much of a professional to do that because I want to do what is right for you." After you have given this explanation, it is not necessary to wait for a reply. *Close the sale by once again asking for the order.*

Dwight Lankford, with Piedmont Marketing in Myrtle Beach, South Carolina, who is the nation's leading recreational time-sharing property salesperson, claims that his success with be-backs is only 2 percent. "Yet, if I go 'all or nothing' with these prospects, my closing ratio is thirty percent," he declares. "With these odds, Piedmont Marketing salespeople offer a built-in first-day discount, ranging between eight hundred to fifteen hundred depending upon the size of the property. Incidentally, this is an attractive incentive considering our average one-week time-sharing sale is approximately seventy-five hundred.

"We have a rule that nobody gets the discount if he doesn't buy on the spot,"Lankford continues. "The key to making this policy effective is that there are no exceptions. *Never!* Even if somebody were to come back the following morning with a certified check in the amount of the price quoted with the first-day discount, it is not acceptable. If one of our people were to say just one time, 'Yes, you can have it for the price I quoted you yesterday,' then it would never be effective again. None of us would ever have the same conviction, and everyone who ever received it would have been made to look like a sucker."

At a certain point, after working for a period of time with a customer to sell a large computer system, IBM's Buck Rodgers gets right to the point by saying: "Look, we have spent a lot of time together, and I clearly understand your problem. I think I have the best answer, so let's you and I proceed and we'll get the equipment in as soon as possible. I suggest we get the order signed and then we'll take the next step."

When faced with a prospect who wants to think it over, Joe Gandolfo says: "No one has a lease on life, and nobody knows when the Lord is going to take you. There is not going to be any additional information available later on that is not available today. Now if you're sincere and truly care, then we need to act immediately. If not, then this conversation is futile because up until now you've neglected to insure your life adequately, and frankly, you have been quite fortunate."

Sometimes, Gandolfo will encounter a prospect who says: "You're really putting the pressure on me, Joe." When this happens, Gandolfo responds: "Well, sure, but if I don't, who will? I'm doing this for your own good."

The hardball selling philosophy advocates that every salesperson must have a no-callback policy. By letting the buyer know where you stand on callbacks, you create a strong sense of urgency to make an immediate decision.

Credibility

On a trip to New York, my wife and I were in the diamond district, shopping to buy her a diamond ring. We stopped in a jewelry store and inquired about an emerald cut in the window. After Bobbie tried on the ring, the salesman asked, "What do you think?"

"I think forty-five thousand is a lot of money for a ring," I answered.

"That's not your price," he said to me. "If you buy it today, you can have it for twelve thousand."

"Twelve thousand!" I exclaimed, shocked by the fact that he had dropped the price by thirty-three thousand without even so much as batting an eyelash.

"Make that ten thousand, if you buy today."

"I don't get it," I said. "Why are you being so generous? What did we do to deserve such a large discount?"

"Nobody buys it for the ticket price," he answered.

"Then why do you mark it forty-five thousand?" I asked.

"Well, every once in a while, some big oilman comes in

here from someplace out West like Oklahoma or Texas and says, 'I'll give you twenty thousand for that ring in the window, and not a cent more.' " After a slight pause, the salesman added, "So, how do you want to pay for it? By check or credit card?"

"I'll give you a thousand for it," I said.

"Are you crazy?" he shouted, losing his composure. "It's a four-carat diamond."

"I know that's a ridiculous price, but to be perfectly honest, I simply can't do business with you. I could never feel confident that you were giving me a legitimate deal after you dropped the price thirty-three thousand and then another quick two grand." With that we walked out. His credibility was gone.

To effectively create a sense of urgency, you must present a *credible* reason why the prospect should buy today. We lost faith in the jewelry salesperson, so under no circumstances was it possible for him to make the sale. And consider a car salesman saying at the end of the season that a particular model equipped with certain options will not later be available; certainly this close would not be effective for the new models just introduced. Likewise, a life insurance agent may have difficulty convincing a young prospect enjoying perfect health to apply immediately before losing his insurability. Prospects have to believe the reasons you offer or there is no urgency to buy.

But if you think about it, there are many good reasons why there is a credible urgency to buy your product. If the need exists, the sooner a prospect's need is fulfilled, the more he benefits by making a buying decision. Your job is to recognize, in each case, where the urgency lies, convince the prospect, and close the sale.

The Home Court Advantage

Like a basketball team spotted an extra six points for the home court advantage, so will you, too, benefit from working in your own habitat rather than that of the customer. As a competitive sporting event can go either way, so can a borderline sale vacillate.

While a salesperson does not typically bring a customer to his turf, there are exceptions. For instance, the sales representative for a huge company such as IBM or Boeing may invite customers to tour company facilities. After all, how else does one give an actual demonstration of a large computer system or a giant aircraft?

Large companies, while more apt to do this, do not hold a monopoly on bringing in customers. You can do it too. As you will learn in this chapter, you do not have to be a subject of *Lifestyles of the Rich and Famous,* nor do your offices have to be palatial, to take advantage of your home court.

Holding Court

In a truly customer-driven organization, the salesperson is king. Every employee's job description should include supporting the selling effort. With everyone being thoroughly sales-oriented, an ideal selling environment exists, one that presents a favorable image to win customers.

The salesman should always be hailed as the company's hero, because without his contribution, there is no employment for anyone else. It has been said that a man's home is his castle, and much the same can be said about a salesperson's office. Nowhere else is he likely to receive more royal treatment than in the presence of his staff and coworkers. The salesperson feels most at ease working with customers in his own domicile. It is natural for him to feel this way because this is where he holds court.

Home Court Demonstrations

Certainly the most obvious advantage for a customer coming to your place of business is that a complete demonstration can be given. Of course, depending upon what you sell, this advantage will vary, and may, in fact, be mandatory. For instance, it isn't possible to transport a large computer system or fifty-ton automobile die cutter to the customer's place of business. To show how products of this nature best operate, the customer must leave his office and come to you to observe an actual demonstration. Otherwise, his source of information is limited to visual presentations that simulate data via such means as brochures, slides, and videotapes.

Even products that are capable of fitting into a traveling case are better presented at your place of business rather than the customer's. A clothing manufacturer's representative may have only a limited amount of space in a cramped buyer's office to show dozens of dress samples. Typically, retail stores place a premium on floor space, so offices commonly are extremely small. Giving a presentation at his company's showroom enables the rep to display each sample to its best advantage. For instance, the home office might use mannequins or even live models in a presentation—methods that can not be used in the buyer's office.

If you plan properly in advance, a home office demonstration will always be better equipped to present your product in an ideal setting. This should be explained to the customer to entice him to be your guest. After all, it also serves to his advantage.

Having Control

On your turf, a controlled environment exists where *you*, not the buyer, take charge. In the prospect's office, he decides what interruptions are permissible during a sales presentation, including which telephone calls are answered, which visitors are seen, and which emergencies get immediate attention. As every salesperson surely knows, an unwanted interruption can throw off his timing and have a devastating effect on closing the sale. In your own office, you are the one with the authority to eliminate all distractions.

Furthermore, as your guest, a customer is apt to be more docile than in his own domain, where he is in control. In your office his subordinates are not present to cater to his every whim, nor are there yes-men on hand to reinforce a weak excuse to procrastinate. Just as your own home turf provides you with a feeling of being in charge, the buyer feels less in control for having been transplanted to a foreign environment.

Bear in mind that nobody ever gets thrown out of his own office by a disagreeable customer! Knowing this, you can be more aggressive, and, when necessary, press your customer for an order. Remember, too, that it is more awkward for a buyer to get up and walk out of your office than to ask you to leave his!

Common Courtesies

As a matter of courtesy, your support staff should be instructed to hold all calls—telephone or otherwise. Barring a true emergency, a visiting customer deserves your full, undivided attention. This is true even more so than in other sales locations because he has taken the time to come to your place of business.

It is surprising to observe salespeople who attend to other business during a sales presentation. It simply makes no sense to give priority to a telephone caller and ignore the customer who is standing in the flesh in your establishment, likely to buy your product. Nevertheless, I constantly witness salespeople excusing themselves from bona fide customers to engage in a telephone conversation with a prospect who at best, has expressed an interest. It is not only rude, but very bad business. Isn't the application of a-bird-in-the-hand thinking appropriate?

It is also poor business for a salesperson to show up late for an appointment when calling on a customer, and it must *never* happen when the customer comes to the seller. Six years ago when I purchased two word processors for my office, I was asked to come to an office equipment company's downtown offices for a demonstration. "Is it possible for your salesperson to come to my offices?" I asked.

"It's far better for you to see several models on display here," I was told. It made sense, and a 1:30 appointment was scheduled.

I arrived on time only to be told that the salesperson would be with me momentarily. At 1:50, he walked into the showroom and introduced himself.

"Wasn't our meeting scheduled for one-thirty?" I said.

"Yes, and I apologize," he replied. "I was downstairs in the cafeteria and the service was atrocious."

"Then you should have walked out without having lunch."

"I beg your pardon?" he asked.

"It's one thing for a salesperson to show up late at the customer's place," I said. "That's bad enough, but at least when that happens, the customer has plenty to do to keep himself occupied. But when the customer comes to see you, it's incredibly rude of you to keep him waiting."

Although I was in the market for two word processors, I didn't buy them from him. When I got back to my office I scheduled an appointment with a competitor and made a $14,000 purchase the following afternoon.

It is quite complimentary to you to be able to receive a customer at your office. By making the trip, he expresses his recognition of you as a professional; in turn, you should extend your utmost courtesy and respect to him. Interestingly, in Japan, a visiting businessperson is treated as a guest of honor and thereby given the most desirable place to sit in a host's office. It is generally the seat with the best view—across from a window or perhaps a fine piece of art. This is a far cry from the advice offered by several previously published American best-sellers that endorse tactics that include having your guest sit facing the blinding sun. Every visiting customer should be treated with the same degree of courtesy you would extend to a guest in your home.

How to Get Them to Come to Your Place

Ideally, a salesperson could set up appointments by inviting prospects to his place of business and schedule them with one appointment following another throughout the entire day. Not only would this be an efficient use of one's time, but a reduction in travel expenses would also materialize.

Of course, a majority of salespeople find it difficult to persuade most prospects to come to their offices, and attracting them in large numbers is strictly wishful thinking. However, it's an attainable ambition to bring in one or two a week, and increase this number to one customer each day over a period of time. Edwin Ellman, one of America's most successful estate planners, estimates that the majority of his total sales volume over the course of a year is derived from business conducted in his offices. Ellman confesses that this is highly unusual in the life insurance field, yet he has been doing it for some twenty-five years. Today, Ellman's Columbus offices are quite elegant, but he points out that this was not always the case. "Early in my career, my offices were quite modest," he states, "but I always had an attractive conference room that I used to work with visiting clients. Even when it represented figures that, perhaps, exceeded what my budget could afford, I had a kitchen in which my secretary or an assistant could prepare a meal. In the beginning, it certainly was not a fancy meal—perhaps a steak or a salad—but I used it as the attraction to get somebody to come to my place. 'Let's have lunch on Tuesday,' I'd say, 'to review your estate planning.' Once I had the lunch date set up, I would add, 'I'll pick you up at eleven-forty-five.'

"When somebody would ask, 'Where are we going for lunch? I'd say, 'It's a surprise, but you are going to love it. I promise you that it will be very private so we can conduct a confidential business conversation without any interruptions.' "

As Ellman's career became more successful, so did the elegance of his lunches. Today, lunch at Ellman & Associates is considered by many Columbusites to be a delightful culinary experience.

Ellman emphasizes that it is not essential to have kitchen facilities. "I realize that not every salesperson can afford this luxury. But it is possible to have lunch delivered by a fine nearby restaurant, or, even better, have some outside establishment cater it. Later, when your business warrants the extra cost, you might want to consider a kitchen."

Joe Gandolfo invites his clients to visit his offices in Lakeland, Florida—at their own expense. "Being fifteen miles from Disney World makes a difference in getting them to come to see me from all over the country." Gandolfo explains. "They spend a day with me and make a mini-vacation out of it. Secondly, I have observed that wealthy people generally don't like doing business locally. In my field, they want the confidentiality, and they don't even like having their employees see somebody from out-of-town come to their offices." Gandolfo also stresses the convenience of having his computers and access to information at his fingertips in his own place of business.

On a much larger scale, IBM often goes much further and invites groups of customers to visit its headquarters. In what are referred to as "customer conferences," IBM hosts meetings that range in size from fifty to a thousand participants. These conferences are designed to provide everyone from product planners to development engineers an opportunity to mix and exchange ideas. At its top-level conferences, IBM conducts Chief Executive Officers Classes, which are meetings running twelve hours a day for five days. The credentials of these guests are quite impressive; they are either presidents or chairmen of the board of companies with annual sales in excess of one billion dollars, presidents of large universities, and top politicians, usually at the level of state governor. These meetings focus on how to improve customers' operations through the use of advanced management techniques and new computer technologies. Despite the VIPs who come to IBM's Poughkeepsie and San Jose facilities to attend these conferences, the demand to attend is so high that there is a waiting list to be included.

While few companies have the prestige of IBM, the principle of inviting customers to your place of business is the same: It is an effective way to sell and, most important, customers are willing to come.

Sell the Team

In general, when a salesperson calls on customers only at their places of business, he is their sole contact with his company. Thus, his company's image is based exclusively on the clients' impressions of one person—him. No matter how wonderful an image a particular salesperson projects, it rarely equals the image presented when customers interact with a team of top-notch people. Although it is possible to transport the entire team to the customers' locations, it is generally better to bring those customers to your home court.

People are always the greatest asset of a business. Through meeting your people, customers realize that they are not doing business with a single person, but an organization. This message is vital to establishing long-term relationships.

Customers must be shown that the strength of your organization lies in its depth. This is essential because they need to be assured that there is adequate backup if ever you are unavailable when needed. After all, individuals get sick, take vacations, retire, and die.

Having experts in your organization who specialize also gives you a strong advantage. At IBM, it is referred to as value-added service. Customers buy more than a little black box when they buy an IBM computer. They are buying a team of technicians and programmers who will make sure that the customer derives the most use out of his computer. At an insurance or real estate agency, team specialists may be CPAs or attorneys. Even in a law firm, depth must be sold to a potential client. For instance, a firm that specializes in business law will stress that it has experts in such areas as securities, real estate, taxation, and labor. It is important for customers to realize that a team of competent people are available *after the sale* if a problem occurs.

The Trimmings of Success

For obvious reasons, having the "right" address helps create the image you want to project. Renting space in a prestigious office building may cost considerably more than a cheap one in a blighted neighborhood, but if you want to attract customers, it is a must. To do otherwise would create an image of hard times, and as I previously discussed, successful people want to do business with other successful people. So, to properly impress first-class customers, first-class offices are extremely valuable.

Not only does this mean a respectable address, but you must also complete your offices with the right furnishings. Unless you are the exception to the rule, it is recommended that you employ the services of a professional interior decorator.

While your capacity to perform is your chief selling point, customers feel more comfortable in well-appointed offices. Did you ever wonder why so many banks have marble floors and walls? After all, marble has nothing to do with the nature of the banking business. However, marble signals a message of permanency—it suggests that the structure will withstand the test of time. What an appropriate image for a bank's trust and bonds departments to relate to customers! Similarly, a life insurance agent wants his clients to know that his company and his agency will be around to provide service for many years into the future. So while a banking or insurance office may be designed to have a traditional look with black walnut veneers and classical decorative molding detail, another office, such as a public relations or advertising firm, may have a modern look to convey a conceptual and futuristic image.

A word of caution: Be careful to avoid overkill. *Excessive* trimmings are considered gaudy and in poor taste. Then too, depending upon the nature of your business, you don't want your customers to think your outrageous overhead is reflected in your prices and passed on to the buyer. To give this impression would be counterproductive. So do things in moderation. Sometimes a sterile but efficient image will appeal to your customers. It is not necessary to invest a fortune to create a good working atmosphere where competent and dedicated people are employed to serve customers. The trimmings of success for one business can be the kiss of death for another. Furthermore, each individual has a different personality, which determines what works best in his or her situation. What must be considered, however, is having a game plan—don't sit back and let the appearance of your office randomly evolve.

Office Billboards

Once you have the customer on your turf, be sure to use everything in your office to your best advantage. While your walls may be nicely decorated, they also represent an overlooked selling tool that can serve as excellent props. In particular, they could be put to good use as billboards to promote you and your company. This is prime space for relating a positive story about you—so get rid of that ugly swordfish you caught eight years ago in the Caribbean. While it may represent a sentimental attachment, the fish is taking up good wall space that could convey an important message. Or even worse, it may be a distraction that could result in an untimely and trivial fish story!

One successful life insurance agent I know has his walls

decorated with awards including his Phi Beta Kappa, Life Member of the Million Dollar Round Table, Chartered Life Underwriter, college diplomas, and dozens of plaques that portray him as a top sales producer for several different companies that he represents. Other awards recognize him for his achievements in community work. "I want my clients to know my achievements, but it would appear boastful for me to talk about them. These are things that I would feel uncomfortable discussing in a client's office, and I'd sound like an egomaniac if I did. But in my office, well, they're just hanging on the wall, so I don't have to say a word about them. I can just keep quiet, and eventually a client will say something like, 'Oh, I see you have an MBA from Harvard,' or 'I never realized you're a certified public accountant.' It gives me a chance to show some humility by nonchalantly replying, 'Yes, I am. Now, we were discussing . . .'"

Again, depending on what you sell and your personality, there are many ways to use your walls to tell a specific message. Joe Girard, for instance, does not believe in having anything on his walls that will distract his customer. He considers photographs of car models to be particularly distracting because they make the buyer think about cars other than the one Girard is selling. He does like newspaper write-ups on his sales records, and he has a photograph of himself taken with former President Gerald Ford. Similarly, Joe Gandolfo's insurance offices are covered wall-to-wall with symbols of recognition he has received in the life insurance field. Gandolfo feels these awards inform his clients that he is a superstar in his field, which, of course, he is.

Other leading salespeople have a different view about what message should be displayed on their walls. Ed Ellman, for example, has also received dozens of awards in recognition of his high life insurance sales, but none are displayed. "It is not my style to announce that I am a supersalesman," he confides.

"I don't want my clients thinking about me in that capacity. I would rather be regarded by them as an adviser. This identity creates a better atmosphere for people to feel comfortable confiding in me, so I personally downplay my role as a salesperson."

Meeting on Neutral Courts

There are times when your meetings with customers will take place at neither their nor your home court. These neutral sites can be such places as restaurants, private clubs, and hotel suites. Oftentimes, neutral locations offer many of the same advantages that your home court does. Here, too, interruptions are reduced, and you can maintain control.

When selecting a meeting place, a key consideration is that business matters can be discussed in privacy—not only do you want to reduce noise and distractions, confidentiality is also vital. An estate planner, for instance, might ask a series of financial questions that a prospect might feel uncomfortable answering within hearing distance of a group at a nearby table. And certainly, a nightclub with loud background music does not create an appropriate business atmosphere. Adequate lighting is also a factor to consider, especially if it is necessary for your customer to view proposals or perhaps visuals. Your selection of a neutral court should be based on its elegance. Bear in mind that hardball selling demands projecting an image of success. Dining out with a customer is not an occasion on which to cut corners. Private clubs have an air of exclusivity and prestige that accomplishes all of the above—privacy, quietness, good lighting, and elegance.

A neutral court may also provide some utilitarian value. For example, the clothing manufacturer's rep might choose his hotel suite as a place to meet with a customer. "I am staying at the Ritz," he tells a buyer, "and I would like you to visit my suite at twelve-thirty on Tuesday afternoon. I'll arrange for lunch to be served upon your arrival. I will have my samples displayed so you can see the entire line. You will be in and out of here in ninety minutes." Rather than working out of several sample cases, this salesperson uses his suite as his showroom. When one is visiting a large city such as Chicago or New York, it can be extremely difficult to physically transport one's merchandise to and from retail stores. The extra cost for a hotel suite can be a bargain compared to out-of-pocket expenses for taxis and valet services. As an added bonus, the superior presentation that is possible in a better setting is likely to result in a larger order.

Trains, Planes, Yachts, and Other Whatnots

Other selling tools used by top salespeople can run the gamut including private railroad cars, corporate jets, deluxe yachts, and magnificent resort homes. Some sales organizations use skyboxes in sports arenas to woo their customers. In case you have never been in one, a skybox can seat twenty people or so, and can come equipped with a private air-conditioned dining room and bar.

The late John W. Galbreath once confided in me, "My Darby Dan Farm is more than my residence. It has an important business function." The Darby Dan Farm is a 4,300-acre ranch located just west of Columbus, Ohio, complete with an airport housing two corporate jets, two racetracks, a golf course, swimming pool, tennis courts, ten-thousand-square-foot party house, and a private zoo. Galbreath, one of America's most prominent real estate developers, pointed out that he routinely brought clients from all over the world to Darby Dan. "Many of my biggest deals were made on the farm," he explained.

Super Hollywood Agent Jay Bernstein uses his residence,

which was once the mansion of Carole Lombard and Clark Gable, as his office. Bernstein's staff includes a full-time chef, who regularly serves delectable meals to his clients. Bernstein readily admits that, as a bachelor, "It would be foolish for me to live in such an enormous home if I did not use it to promote my business."

While such things as skyboxes and large estates are selling tools of the superrich, I bring them to your attention to emphasize that there are virtually no limits to those "extras" that can be used to add a few points to the home team's scoreboard. Just remember that, while it takes money (or at least the appearance of money) to make money, there are definite limitations. Be certain to apply sound business judgment or your expenditures will devour your bottom line.

Many of the country's most successful salespeople are taking advantage of their home court, yet it is still a dimension of selling that is commonly overlooked. Too often, lesser salespeople think it is a technique reserved only for the affluent. But, for the record, leading sales producers do not start their careers at the top. They get there by working hard and working *smart.* And it is smart to use the home court to your advantage.

It's Not Over 'til It's Over

A salesperson should never limit himself to a single attempt at closing. If the first attempt fails, one must continue with the sales presentation and attempt again to close. And it does not stop at a second rejection. A successful salesperson must follow through with another execution, again and again. The hardball philosophy is based on the premise, "If at first you don't succeed, try, try again." Above all else, a hardball salesperson is tenacious.

To accept "no" as a final answer is tantamount to submitting to mediocrity. Success depends on the ability to convert nos into yeses. In part, this is the very nature of a career in selling. There is a distinct difference between selling a product and merely writing up the order. If sales closings only occurred when there was no resistance, high sales commissions would cease to exist.

Don't Interpret No to Mean No Sale!

During my extensive interviews with the top salespeople in the U.S., I observed a common denominator shared by all of them: "They refuse to interpret no as *"I am not going to buy."* Instead, they consider it only a minor obstacle, one that provides a thrill when a sale is subsequently closed. Success rests on having the tenacity to accept this temporary setback as a challenge and to press on until the prospect consents. The real test of a hardball salesperson is closing a sale *after* a prospect says no.

For the most part, buyers have a natural tendency to say no during a sales presentation. This happens because the initial reaction is not to buy every product offered during every sales call. Imagine an individual who did buy everything. It would be only a matter of time before he faced financial ruin! You must therefore acknowledge the existence of a built-in resistance. A person may express a sometimes convincing motive to reject your proposal to buy. It is essential to realize that although a prospect appears reluctant, you should not literally interpret this as an absolute disinterest.

Furthermore, a prospect may say "no" more than once during the course of a sales presentation. Just as hearing it once is not a call for discouragement, neither should several nos be construed as failure. In fact, the consensus among leading sales experts is that seven nos are acceptable before one can conclude that a sale can't be closed. However, since every presentation has a different set of circumstances, each must be handled on its own merit. This means that frequently more than seven closing attempts are necessary. Taking a nothing-to-lose-and-everything-to-gain approach, the hardball salesperson persists.

The Thin Line

Some time ago, after making several attempts to close a large group insurance sale, I sensed my prospect felt somewhat uncomfortable with the high pressure I had exerted. "Do you know what?" I interjected out of nowhere. "I have a feeling that you're a little annoyed because I have been pressing you so hard to make a decision."

"You got that right," he said with a wry smile.

"Well, I just hope you appreciate it," I replied. "Because I'm not enjoying this any more than you are."

My comment provoked a slight rise of the prospect's eyebrows.

"I want you to know," I continued, "there is a thin line between being a pest and having persistence. Now, while I have demonstrated my tenacity in order to convince you to make what I consider an obvious decision that will solve your problem, you may not fully appreciate it today. But someday you will. You see, it is this same brand of tenacity that, as your agent, will serve you when a dispute over a claim with the insurer arises." To justify my remark, I added, "It doesn't matter what insurance company an agent represents; in a large group case like yours, inevitably a borderline claim will require a tenacious agent to go to bat for the client. And when this happens, you are going to find out what you felt was a slightly overbearing quality is not so bad after all."

"Oh no," he exclaimed, "I admire your stick-to-itiveness. Please don't apologize for it."

While I was not apologizing, I was pleased to hear what I accepted as his consent.

Several years later, I closed another big sale the same way. This time, I was convincing an executive of one of the world's largest industrial companies that I should be chosen as the one to write its official story. I was competing against several other writers for a book destined to be a best-seller, and I felt somewhat unsure about whether I would get the assignment. The competition was stiff. After making a dozen or so calls to press for a decision in my favor, I borrowed the line from my insurance days and said: "You know, a thin line exists between being a pest and having persistence. Now while I have demonstrated my tenacity in order to convince you that I should be selected to write the book, I hope you recognize this as a positive quality. In fact, it is this very quality that the chosen author must possess in order to write this particular book. So please view it as one of my strengths rather than an annoyance. A tenacious writer is essential, especially during this project because it necessitates conducting a series of interviews with the company's highest-ranking executives. As you know, most of them have big egos—a Mr. Milquetoast writer could not deal with them. They would eat him for lunch. You need me *because* I'm tenacious."

This remark generated a favorable response, and I always felt it was the issue that swayed the pendulum in my favor over the other writers. Once again, my writing career was the beneficiary of my selling talent.

Having an Awareness of False Objections

Sometimes a prospect is reluctant to express his real objection and, instead, gives a false one as his reason for not buying. Unless you are able to convince him why his real objection is unwarranted, the chances are slim that you will close the sale. Simply bombarding him with facts irrelevant to his true objection will not win him over. This is illustrated in the following example.

Mark is trying to convince his girlfriend, Lisa, to spend the afternoon with him sailing on the local river. Lisa can't swim and has a strong fear of drowning, but she is embarrassed to admit it to Mark. Instead, Lisa says that she does not want to go sailing because the river is polluted and represents a potential health hazard.

No matter how hard Mark attempts to convince her that there are pollution controls which assure the purity of the water, he will not persuade her to join him for a day of sailing. Although he may offer intelligent and convincing reasons that the water is unpolluted, her fears of drowning will remain intact. Of course, by chance, he may mention that it does not matter that the water is polluted because his boat is constructed so it can't tip over. While this rebuttal is directed at the contaminated water issue, it also solves the fear-of-drowning issue.

As illustrated above, and in selling too, it is sometimes possible to "get lucky" and satisfy the true objection with a rebuttal that is intended to counteract another reason for not buying. The odds of this happening, however, are not good. In Mark's case, he must convince Lisa that her fears of drowning are unfounded, and to accomplish this, he must first be aware that this is her real reason for turning down his offer to go sailing.

To recognize a false objection, you must carefully observe a prospect's reaction to your explanation; if he continues to balk at sound reasons for buying, you are probably barking up the wrong tree. When this happens, you may consider confronting him directly with : "Sir, I have a strong suspicion that there is something you have not told me that is preventing you from buying today. I want you to tell me about it."

Another sign that a prospect is not expressing his true feelings is when he continually states a new objection each time you provide a logical rebuttal that he can't dispute. In this situation, you can assume that nobody has so many bona fide excuses; there must be something that he is hiding. Here too, a direct confrontation is appropriate.

Objections Are Requests for Information

As stated previously, many people have a natural tendency not to buy although they are prime prospects who need your product. Consequently, they will challenge you to convince them to buy; their intentions are to make you sell them, not simply write up their orders. These challenges are offered in the form of objections that are not to be considered negative reactions. While objections discourage an ordinary salesperson, you must perceive them as requests for information, as if the prospect were saying: "Convince me I should buy your product."

Interestingly, if there is not the slightest trace of dissension throughout the course of a sales presentation, it is probable that the prospect has no interest whatsoever in your product. For example, Mark Phelps, a swimming pool salesman, encounters no objections from Pearl and Anne Arbor, to whom he is trying to sell a deluxe pool, because the two spinster sisters haven't the slightest interest in purchasing one.

"This is the finest filter system in the industry," Phelps states.

"Isn't that nice," Anne comments good-naturedly.

"It is virtually maintenance-free," he emphasizes.

"Oh really?" Pearl says with a congenial smile.

And later, as Phelps attempts to close the sale, he explains, "Until the end of the week, we have a special—you only have to pay three percent financing changes. Or, if you would rather write out a check for the full amount, I will give you a one-thousand-dollar cash rebate."

The Arbor sisters have no reaction, so Phelps adds, "Would you prefer our finance plan or would you rather take the cash rebate?"

"Oh, we have no interest in either," Anne answers.

"Is there something I failed to explain to you?" Phelps asks.

"Oh no,"Pearl replies."You did a marvelous job and my sister and I gratefully appreciate having you stop by to see us."

No matter how long Phelps continues with his sales presentation, his efforts are in vain because the Arbor sisters are simply not interested in owning a swimming pool.

Conversely, in the case of a presentation made to a party who does have an interest, Phelps is likely to encounter some objections that he can interpret as positive signs. For instance, a prospect states: "My main concern about having a swimming pool is that I don't want to be a slave to it. I don't have the time to spend a half hour every day removing debris."

This comment allows Phelps to interject: "The beauty about owning this pool is that it does not require you to do that kind of dreadful work. Of course, a few years ago, that's the way it was. People would spend hours cleaning their pools." Then, he goes on to explain the new technology that has made major improvements in the industry.

When you encounter the weak candidate who never makes a comment during a sales presentation, there are ways to turn the presentation around. You must get the client to talk, since head nods or silence frequently mean that the prospect has nothing to say because he has no interest. In order to get a presentation of this nature back on track, you must ask leading questions that invite the prospect to participate. You must solicit his involvement. The more he comments—even through the expression of objections—the more he will reveal what you need to know to close the sale, if it can be closed.

Be Equipped with an Arsenal of Closes

After a prospect says no, you must continue to provide more reasons why he should buy your product, and each time, follow through with an attempt to close the sale. It is sometimes necessary for this procedure to be repeated—the sale isn't over until it's over. Since many attempts may be required, you must be equipped with an arsenal of different closes. This does not imply that you should never repeat a close during the same sales presentation. Sometimes it may be appropriate to repeat a close, but, in general, a variety of closes is more effective. The danger with the repetition of a particular closing technique is that it may be recognized by the prospect and cause him to think: "Here comes another attempt to close." When you are too obvious, your efforts appear contrived and lack credibility.

When a prospect expresses an objection at the close of the sale, you must answer it in detail. However, having done so, you should not anticipate anyone saying: "Now that you made that point, I will buy your product." It doesn't work that way. Instead, upon overcoming an objection, you must automatically assume that the prospect has accepted your reasons for buying, and close the sale with an assumptive close as if he voiced his consent and said: "I am now ready to make the right buying decision." Although I mentioned earlier that the assumptive close is overworked and consequently not a good choice for making an initial closing attempt, I do approve its usage following your response to an objection.

For instance, a life insurance agent might encounter some resistance when closing a sale. Then, upon believing he has satisfactorily overcome the prospect's objection, assume the sale by asking, "What is your middle initial?" By saying, "J," the prospect has, in effect, consented for the agent to complete the application. By writing in the answer to each question, the prospect is agreeing to purchase the policy because there is no other purpose for providing such information.

If the prospect continues to balk, the agent must continue to state additional reasons why a decision to buy must be made immediately. If the prospect expresses a desire to contact other insurance companies, the agent needs to provide more information to convince him that no other insurer provides a more competitive policy. Thereupon, the agent should attempt to close the sale again by saying: "I am scheduling you for a physical examination on Tuesday at three o'clock with Dr. Hyde." Here too, he should not ask the prospect for his permission to be examined. He must assume that the prospect is agreeable and it is no longer necessary to investigate other companies' policies.

Let's say, however, that the prospect remains unconvinced and still does not agree to be scheduled for an examination. Upon providing him with additional reasons for buying, the agent may elect to use this same close again. "What is a good time for me to set you up with that examination on Tuesday?" he asks, repeating the same assumption. Some repetition is acceptable although a score of other assumptive closes could also be used.

"I need to put down your beneficiary. What is your spouse's full name?"

"Do you want to use your home or work address for billing purposes?"

"Do you want to pay annually or semiannually?"

Assumptive closes do not have to be in the form of questions. You can also make assumptive statements such as :

"Okay this line right here so the company has permission to obtain medical information from your doctor."

"Make out your check to the company for this amount."

"I want to congratulate you on your wise decision."

Of course, the above life insurance agent does not have to use an assumptive close. Instead, he could execute a number of different closes such as those discussed in Chapter 7, "Creating a Sense of Urgency." For instance, he could stress that by delaying the buying decision, the prospect could experience a change in health and become uninsurable—or worse, the prospect could die unexpectedly. Then too, the agent could cast doubts about the prospect's insurability and cause him to wonder if he could qualify for the policy. And in still another close, he could state: "I am sorry but I do not make callbacks," and with this statement, explain why it is imperative for the prospect to make an immediate decision.

It doesn't matter what product you sell: you are never limited to having only a single closing technique. Your ultimate success rests upon your ability to draw upon your reserves when confronted with resistance. Of course, these reserves do not only include having a variety of closing techniques; you must also come equipped with a vast amount of product knowledge. This is true because you can never be certain about the kind of objection someone might express that may require specific knowledge about a particular aspect of your business. In a delicate, teetering selling situation, the sale can go down the tubes if you tell a prospect, "I can't answer that and will have to get back to you when I find out." It is essential to be equipped with the necessary knowledge and closing techniques. The more artillery you bring to the table, the better are your chances of a successful closing of the sale.

"There Must Be Something I Inadvertently Failed to Tell You . . ."

When a prospect is still undecided, a good close is to say with a puzzled expression on your face: "There must be something

I inadvertently failed to tell you. I must apologize. Now, let's see what I could have left out . . ." This comment implies that a reasonable person would buy if he or she had all of the facts. It suggests that there is no logical reason why anyone would *not* buy knowing the benefits and value of the product.

What's more, the prospect is caught off guard. A typical reaction is for the client to automatically think about what he might have missed—why he should have bought instead of rejecting the seller's offer. When he does, he is selling himself.

"I don't think you left anything out," he reluctantly says.

"I'm certain I had to," the salesperson says. "Now let's see. Oh yes, let me tell you about . . ." and he then elaborates on a particular strong selling point or covers a new subject altogether.

"Are You Feeling High-Pressured?"

"Are you feeling a little high-pressured?" I will ask a prospect who is becoming somewhat uncomfortable as a result of my hardball tactics.

"Yes," he will respond. "As a matter of fact, I am."

"Good," I always reply. "Because this is exactly how I want you to feel. I'm doing it for your own good because if I don't, you might fail to make the right decision. So I want to do everything in my power to avoid having you make a mistake. Someday, you will thank me for doing this."

Saying this to a prospect from out of the clear blue sky almost always generates a favorable reaction. I find it most effective during one of those difficult sales presentations that has put both the prospect and me through the ringer several times. It seems to break the tension as well as making a valid point.

Single-Purpose Selling

As a hardball salesperson, you must be goal-oriented and possess a single purpose. That purpose is to close the sale. You must not allow any distraction to throw you off course, and this includes any and all objections expressed by a prospect.

Too often, a protesting prospect will derail a salesperson with a negative comment that will cause the sales presentation to go astray. This sometimes creates confusion, and, as a consequence, the salesperson fails to make another attempt to close the sale. Each time you encounter resistance you must meet it head-on and continue to follow up with another close. This process must sometimes be repeated several times during a single presentation until a transaction occurs. The real selling actually begins when the customer puts up resistance, so keep yourself focused on your single purpose for being there. Your mission is to close the sale! It does not end until you accomplish it.

In the following chapter, you will discover that a hardball salesperson has an even bigger ongoing mission. You will soon find out that it is *never* over!

10

Owning Customers

It is probable that the suggestion of owning customers will shock anyone not familiar with the theory behind hardball selling. However, having read this far, it should not come as a surprise to you.

Of course nobody literally owns anybody. Accounts you open are, in fact, yours; nonetheless, putting new business on the books is just the beginning. Once you get an order you must earn the right to keep it. And, unless you provide your customers with outstanding service, somebody who will is going to take them away.

The real selling does not begin until *after* the sale. While this is not intended to underestimate the talent and effort required to make an initial sale, you must generate repeat business or your sales career will stagnate. Merely opening *x* amount of accounts each year and not retaining them is not progress. I pity the salespeople in this world who fail to realize the value of servicing customers, because, without this essential element of the selling process, advancement in one's sales career is not feasible. Selling and service must go hand in hand.

The first two to three years during the beginning stages of

a sales career require a huge investment of time and hard work making cold calls. This the price one must pay to build a business with a solid clientele. But, it will not be so tedious thereafter if your customers are satisfied with your outstanding service. By then, an estimated 80 percent of your sales will come from current customers and prospects they refer to you. There is no alternative but to service your customers; otherwise the consequences are predictably disastrous. When a salesman fails to generate repeat orders and referrals from satisfied customers, selling becomes an extremely difficult vocation—a dreaded career—one requiring a salesman to pound the pavement day in and day out, year after year.

The name of the game is service, service, service. Give your customers so much service that they will feel guilty even thinking about doing business with somebody else. Joe Girard tells his new customers: "I hope the car you just bought from me turns out to be a lemon, because I'm gonna turn that lemon into lemonade. And I'll give you so much service, I'm gonna own you for the rest of your life." Yes, owning customers is what every hardball salesperson strives to do. But you can own only those customers who want to be owned because they believe in you. You must earn the right to own them by winning their allegiance.

Think Long-Term

Initially, your number one objective is to close the sale, because *nothing happens until a sale is closed.* For obvious reasons, if you do not make the sale in the first place, you will never have the opportunity to service a prospect. The initial closing of the sale, however, should only be considered your *short-term* objective. You must think long-term and strive to build a substantial block of customers whom you will continue to sell throughout the duration of your career. You own this block of customers, and the larger it is, the more success you will have. Only in certain unusual circumstances does a salesperson have a single large account such as IBM or Ford. But one or many, the concept is the same. In each instance, it is essential to provide superior service so you can generate many sales from satisfied customers; the initial order is only the tip of the iceberg compared to the volume of sales that can grow geometrically from it.

For example, when a customer buys an automobile from a salesman, it represents, say, a fifteen-thousand-dollar sale. But, when the salesman provides excellent service and the buyer purchases many more cars from him over a period of the next twenty-five years, hundreds of thousands of dollars in sales may be realized. And, when that satisfied car owner refers several members of his family as well as friends to the salesman and they also become long-term customers, the initial sale can become an account worth a million dollars or more!

All great sales careers are built like this, and, for that matter, so are great companies. In mature industries such as automobile manufacturing, companies concentrate on market share. To these firms, market share is more revered than annual earnings. This is true because the higher the percentage of a market a company captures, the more future business it can realize down the road as a result of repeat business from satisfied customers. In the past, many American managers were smitten with "quarteritis," a short-sighted attitude affliction that was driven by quarterly profits. They were more interested in providing a steady flow of dividends to shareholders than in the future health of the company. But it is of little value to achieve a 20 percent increase in today's dividend only to be out of business five years from now.

Likewise, many salespeople are overly focused on new sales; so much so that, once they get a signed order, they think their work is finished. They fail to provide the necessary follow-up service to satisfy the customer's needs. These sales-people may generate decent commissions on first-time orders, but those sales are small potatoes in comparison to what would result if contented customers placed reorders again and again. Plus, the no-service salespeople eventually exhaust their territories; their poor reputations make them unwelcome visitors the next time around. As a hardball salesperson, you must be committed to acquiring a large market share of the customers in your territory, and this can only be achieved by providing extraordinary service. While it may take a herculean effort in the short run, and often require you to work overtime during the early stages of your career, it will eventually pay big dividends. Those new accounts will become loyal customers—they will belong to you.

A case in point is the success of the Japanese, a result of their emphasis on valuing market share rather than short-term profits. There is an obvious reason why this industrious people have become obsessed with market share. Japan is a land of limited natural resources; it is an overcrowded nation about the size of California with a population of 122 million. With its jagged, mountainous terrain, only 17 percent of its land is habitable. Its population density is 318 people per square kilometer, which is roughly fifteen times greater density than the United States—if Japan had the same population density as the U.S., there would only be eight million people living in Japan. The high population density explains, in part, why Japan is considered the world's most competitive marketplace. In order to survive, salespeople must provide superior service; the nation's fiercely competitive society demands it. Those in Japan who do not provide service fall by the wayside. The Japanese are patient and willing to sacrifice short-term profits in their quest for gaining market share. Evidently, this philosophy works quite well, as witnessed by the enormous success they have enjoyed in recent years. Our domestic companies must meet the challenge the Japanese have brought to our home soil. We, too, must think long-term. This long-term philosophy is compatible with good hardball selling. It is also what is lacking in unscrupulous salespeople, the hucksters who take the customer's money with promises of service, only to disappear after the sale.

Overcoming Buyer's Remorse

It is true that when you sell hardball, you run a higher-than-normal risk of having a customer develop buyer's remorse. As its name implies, buyer's remorse is the second thoughts that occur following a presentation, and its frequency is more prevalent when high pressure is exerted to close a sale. Assuming that you are planning to do business with the customer on a continual basis, you must not leave him with vacillating feelings about his buying decision.

The first and most obvious step to avoid buyer's remorse is to say: "I sincerely appreciate your confidence in me, sir, and I want to congratulate you on making an excellent decision." Always remember that everyone likes to be thanked for his business. After all, chances are that he could have bought your product from another salesperson. By praising the buyer, you confirm that he made a good choice.

Secondly, a thank-you letter should be sent to the buyer within twenty-four hours after the sale. This reassures him that you are a legitimate businessperson. Bearing in mind that you applied some high pressure in closing the sale, the letter catches off guard an otherwise suspicious buyer who may have been thinking that you sold him a bill of goods. Of course, expressing your gratitude is also a matter of common courtesy, which every professional salesperson should automatically extend.

A few days after the letter goes out, a follow-up telephone

call is in order. Here too, you might simply want to thank him for his business, or maybe pass along some additional information that you previously did not mention. For example, a computer sales rep calls to tell a new customer: "I checked with our service department and we can install your system at the end of the week." A life insurance agent tells his client: "Congratulations. You passed the physical examination you took on Tuesday." And a real estate agent calls to say: "I just checked with three banks, and I have some information to review with you about obtaining a mortgage on your new home." In each instance, the salesperson starts off the buyer/seller relationship with a service, even if it is simply a matter of communicating some minor information. Furthermore, he is demonstrating his conscientiousness *after* the sale. This is in contrast to the way the high-pressure salesperson is perceived by the general public. The sooner the buyer knows you are sincere about providing outstanding service, the less he will be overwhelmed by buyer's remorse.

An Important Transition

Hardball selling necessitates high-pressure tactics to close sales. And, while this is what it takes to get initial orders, these tactics cannot be used repeatedly on customers. The law of diminishing returns is applicable—high-pressure selling will wear thin and cause resentment. In an industry where a salesperson contacts regular customers, a transition must be made to develop long-lasting relationships with these clients. For example, a salesperson who sells merchandise such as pharmaceutical articles, medical supplies, or automotive parts often makes a series of weekly calls on his accounts. While the first order might have been induced by high-pressure selling, eventually the salesperson concentrates on being service-driven rather than sales-driven.

To make the transition, you put on a second hat with the customer—your service hat. Once you get the first order, you must then work ever harder to keep it. Buck Rodgers applies this thinking to the selling of IBM computer systems: "Getting the order may be the easiest thing of all, even though you had to go through the long process of justification. But since a lot of our equipment is leased, it's only going to stay with the customer as long as we keep him satisfied. So the salesperson must keep going back to that customer saying: 'Here's a new product. Here's a new technique. Here's a new application. Here's something I think may save you an hour on the machine.' And boy, is this follow-up activity important! It's a continuing process. We use two words together: 'Sell-Install,' never one without the other. At IBM we say, 'Nothing was ever sold until it is properly installed; nothing is ever installed until it is properly sold.' "

It doesn't matter what you sell. Your product can be computers, heavy machinery, insurance, or advertising specialties. You cannot keep calling on the same people and continually apply high pressure on them. Repeat orders will be placed as a result of the quality of your product and the service you provide. A manufacturing rep who sells a line of furniture, for example, will soon lose his credibility if his merchandise sits and collects dust in the retailer's store. After receiving an initial order, the rep has simply taken the first small step and now he must perform. There are many value-added services he can provide that increase his worth as a salesperson. For instance, he can make recommendations to the retailer on such matters as the proper display of his line of furniture, give advice on advertising and tips about selling it. His involvement may include conducting sales meetings with the store's salespeople to educate them on the quality and value of his goods. He may even work on the floor and sell his merchandise to the store's customers! When a manufacturer's rep lands a new account based on how well his line will sell on a retail level, the rep must back his words with action. The more involved he is *after the sale,* the more likely it will be that reorders will follow.

Little Touches

A twenty-five-year-old man told me that he sends a single rose to his girlfriend because he cannot afford to send flowers by the dozen. "One rose seems to be more effective than any other number less than a dozen," he claims. "If I sent just a few roses, she might think I was too cheap to send a dozen. A single rose, however, is a nice touch that lets her know I care for her and want her to know that I care. It works all the time!"

While I am not suggesting sending a single rose to your customers, there is an important lesson here. People sincerely appreciate a little thoughtful act, and sometimes, because it is not pretentious, it generates more good will than something more costly that smacks of ostentatiousness.

Often, it is the little day-in, day-out deeds a salesperson does for a customer that build a lasting long-term relationship. These can range from the prompt return of a telephone call to the delivery of a requested brochure. Or it may be always being prompt for appointments. This brand of reliable follow-through relays the important message to a customer that you are conscientious and reliable. Conversely, if you lack follow-through, it is probable that people will think: "If I can't rely on this salesman to do small things, I certainly can't depend on him for something major when I really need his service." Rarely are long-term customers won over by one sweeping giant-sized deed, but rather a series of seemingly insignificant ones. When customers are asked why they are loyal to so-and-so, they often reply: "It's hard to explain. I suppose I just feel comfortable doing business with him." The reason it is difficult for them to define their feelings is because the important touches are, in fact, so minor that a customer can't clearly identify them. Or won't. The buyer of a five-million-dollar life insurance policy would feel foolish saying: "Oh, I bought it from my agent because he sends me a card on my birthday and mails me interesting articles that he cuts out of magazines and newspapers."

Going That Extra Mile

While it is the little day-to-day considerations that count, there are also those times when an all-out effort is required. Nobody is expected to operate in overdrive on a continuous basis, but every now and then it is necessary.

For instance, a computer salesperson might have to work overtime, perhaps putting in a long weekend with his company's systems engineers to guarantee the installation, so the customer's system is in operation by Monday morning. Likewise, after the sale has been consummated, a life insurance agent might put in a few extra hours reviewing the policy with the client's CPA and attorney. As a result of some changes in the policyholder's personal life, the agent might be requested to review the same policy the following year. Or perhaps a flood or fire causes the destruction of the book-keeping records of a retail store, so a salesperson has to spend several days helping with an inventory. While these examples of extra service might appear to be above and beyond the call of duty, they are not. Every salesperson must consider going that extra mile as part of his job description, and be on constant standby to do whatever is necessary to serve customers. As an old French proverb says: "A man can run a long distance after he is tired."

Keeping in Touch

No treatment of customers is more thoughtless than to "sell 'em and forget 'em." When people are treated this way, they realize that the salesperson's only interest is to make a commission on the sale; he has no interest in what is best for them. It makes people feel used and abused. As a result, no customer loyalty is built, only feelings of resentment and apprehension.

So, in addition to the immediate phone calls and follow-through letters that I recommend to overcome buyer's remorse, keeping in touch with prospects must continue. Even with thousands of clients spread across fifty states, Joe Gandolfo communicates with each of them on a steady basis. "I shower them with monthly news bulletins on tax planning," he says. "And I call every client once a year to review his or her estate planning. Additionally, my assistants are always calling my clients. I have a WATS line and am constantly encouraging them to call me. Furthermore, I tell them I am on call twenty-four hours a day, 365 days a year. No matter where I am in the United States, I will return every single call each evening before retiring." Gandolfo insists on making himself accessible to his clients. "I never play games with them, like having my secretary say that I am in conference. When people call, I make a point of taking every call even though as many as thirty to forty come in every day."

Many salespeople have a tendency to insulate themselves from customer contact after the initial sale is made; they hide behind layers of receptionists and, when complaints are voiced, have assistants and low-echelon people respond. Behavior of this nature infuriates customers and stifles long-term relationships. It is no wonder some salespeople have a reputation for "always being there to sell you but never being around when you need them." Top salespeople insist on receiving all calls, and they handle their customers' problems personally.

Keeping in touch through personal contact is unquestionably the best way to communicate with customers because it generates two-way communication. However, constant reminders such as monthly newsletters are also an effective method of letting people know that you're thinking about them. My favorite reminder is one Ari Deshe, president of Employee Benefit Systems, uses. He sends Fruit of the Month baskets to his key customers. "Each month, I mail a beautifully packaged basket of delicious fresh fruit to the president, personnel director, and payroll clerk of each of my major accounts," Deshe explains. "The baskets are sent to their homes just a day or two before the monthly premium notices arrive at the office. The package is a luxury item and something that most people probably would not buy for themselves. The entire family enjoys this gift, and more importantly, becomes accustomed to receiving it. Every month they look forward to it as their last month's supply runs out. It serves as a constant reminder to each of my customers that I am thinking about him or her." And when your customers believe that you are thinking about them, they, in turn, will think about you.

Keeping a Customer Profile

Although he was a mathematical genius, Albert Einstein was known to have a poor memory for trivial matters such as phone numbers and addresses. He claimed he did not have to remember numbers or other information that could be recorded in his files, so felt no need to tax his brain unnecessarily.

As the number of your accounts increases, the more you

need to know about your customers. But, like Einstein, there is no reason for you to attempt to memorize the unnecessary. Instead, you should keep a file on each account. Then only a quick glance will be needed to brief yourself on what you need to know before contacting the customer. The file can include such things as names of other employees, spouse, other family members, birthdate, special interests (golf, woodcarving, rock collecting, etc.), dates and sizes of previous orders, and so forth.

Martin Shafiroff keeps detailed profiles of his clients on index cards onto which he adds brief notes of all conversations. For instance, if somebody expresses an interest in stocks with high yields, this information is recorded to remind Shafiroff to include it in his next telephone conversation with that person. Also listed on the card are the sizes of past transactions, prior investment experiences, and so on. Shafiroff's files always include the client's secretary's name; secretaries are impressed that he makes an effort to remember them. He claims that some of the most difficult gatekeepers become his allies simply because he calls them by name several weeks or months after his initial contact. Evidently, it leaves quite an impression!

Depending on the nature of your business, you might want to keep a profile on each of your customers. Profiles can be any length and include some very detailed information that contains personal and business information. Some life insurance agents call on each of their clients once a year to update their profiles. An estate planner explains: "In order to properly serve my clients, I must record changes that occur during the year regarding such matters as fluctuations in net worth, earnings, property, marital status, and so forth."

Customers generally react favorably to a salesperson who makes the effort to update their files. It gives them a feeling of security—they know they're in good hands. . . .

Repeat Business

At age forty-two, after a six-year bout with cancer, my wife, Bobbie, died on May 5, 1983. I was devastated. Three months later, I was still suffering my first and only case of writer's block and had not written a single page. My good friend and agent Al Zuckerman called me.

"You have to get on with your life and your writing," he advised me.

"I'd like to, Al, and I'm racking my brains trying to come up with a book idea, but I can't seem to do it. It seems like every idea I have has been written about already."

"Why not go back to the basics," Zuckerman suggested. "Your early books were about selling, and that's the subject you know best. So write a new book on selling. There is always a need for a good book on this subject."

"Come to think of it," I said, half to myself, "I've always wanted to write a book about the perfect sales presentation."

"Tell me about it," he said.

"I would need to spend several days in the field with the world's top salespeople in various fields, and after observing them in action, I would take the best selling techniques of each salesperson and incorporate their gems into a perfect sales presentation."

"Sounds good," he said. "Do it."

Following my conversation with Zuckerman, I wrote down the names of five people whom I planned to contact about their participation in the book: Joe Gandolfo, the world's number one insurance agent; Martin Shafiroff, the world's top stockbroker; and Buck Rodgers, IBM's vice president of marketing. All three were featured in my book *Ten Greatest Salespersons*, which was published in 1978. I also contacted Mary Kay Ash, the dynamic founder and chairman of the board of Mary Kay Cosmetics whom I had interviewed when

I authored *The Entrepreneurs,* published in 1980. The fifth person was Bettye Hardeman, America's top residential real estate salesperson, whom I profiled in *The Real Estate People,* also published in 1980.

My first call was to Shafiroff, with whom I had coauthored *Successful Telephone Selling in the '80s,* released in 1982. Shafiroff said that he would be delighted to be in *The Perfect Sales Presentation.* My next call was to Gandolfo.

"It sounds like a winner, Bob," Gandolfo told me. "But before you do that book, I've been negotiating with Harper & Row to do a book about selling, and I would like you to coauthor it with me. Do my book first and then I'll be in your book."

So, for the next three months, working day and night, I wrote a book with Gandolfo titled *How to Make Big Money Selling.* It was great to be writing again, and I quickly recovered from my case of writer's block!

Afterward, I called Mary Kay Ash, and she agreed to participate in my book.

Next, I called Buck Rodgers.

"This is quite a coincidence," Rodgers said. "I was just about to call you. I've been contemplating writing a book about my marketing career at IBM, and I'd like to ask you for some advice."

"First, do you think there's a book in me?" he asked.

"I have no doubt that there are volumes of books in you," I replied in all sincerity.

"Secondly, I have never written a book, so do you have any suggestions on a writer for me to contact?"

"How about me?" I asked.

"My first choice, Bob. But I didn't think you would be interested."

"Are you kidding? It will be a best-seller. And I would be honored to work with you."

It took a year to write *The IBM Way,* and it was published

in late 1986. Not only was it a best-seller in the United States, but it was published in ten different languages and made the best-seller lists in England and Japan.

Although Bettye Hardeman apparently was not interested in writing a book, she graciously agreed to be in *The Perfect Sales Presentation.* After writing two books, I finally was able to begin my work on one book idea that became four books! The book was dedicated to Bettye, Buck, Joe, Marty, and Mary Kay.

The point of this story is that, over a period of years, these five people had become my close friends. After I had interviewed them for previous books, I kept in close contact with them. Not only did I call them regularly, but every time I wrote a book, I always sent a complimentary copy to each of them. Every time I read a magazine or newspaper article about one of them, I sent it to them. I remembered each of them with Christmas cards, and so on. In time, I had cultivated beautiful friendships with each of them, which I truly value.

Just as I routinely did with clients during my insurance career, I built long-term relationships with these people. While I did not do it with any thought of someday selling them anything, these relationships certainly paid off. As a matter of routine, every salesperson should keep in constant contact with his customers. This is how great careers are built in every field.

Let the World Know You for Your Exceptional Service

IBM spent millions of dollars on its advertising campaign, which simply said: *IBM means service.* Of course, it is one thing to say it and another to mean it. Simply giving lip service to good service without the delivery is bound to someday come back to haunt you. However, IBM does give exceptional service, so the company has earned the right to broadcast it.

IBM is an impressive example of a company that strives for excellence in serving its customers, and, as a consequence, has become the number one leader in its industry throughout the world. The revenues generated by IBM's domestic service run high enough to rank the company in the top one hundred companies of the Fortune 500 listing. Just as IBM has earned its reputation for service excellence, so must you be recognized in your field.

It is important to let people know you do, in fact, give outstanding service. To do this, you must tell them! Rich Port, who for years has been the top residential realtor in Chicago, told me: "Whenever you find a frustrated, disgruntled house seller, it's because he hasn't been told what's taking place with the sale of his home. It's usually just plain bad communication! A client should never, I repeat *never*, have to call the salesman to find out what's happening. A professional salesperson keeps in constant contact with his client. He'll call and tell him everything that's going on. 'We just received a mortgage commitment on your property this morning. We can get so many dollars for so many years.' Perhaps he'll call back on the same day and say, 'I suggest that you keep the lights on in your living room, the ones on the end tables. Is eight P.M. okay for tonight?' 'Today we submitted your home to the multiple listing service. Tomorrow a photographer is coming out to take a picture of the house.' Or another call might be, 'Say, I just wrote this ad last night. Will you help me before I submit it to the newspapers? Let me read it to you.' If there is nothing to call about, then there is something wrong with the salesman—it means he is not doing anything. The secret is to keep in constant touch with the client. Let him know what is happening. The typical real estate agent does a lot more to merchandise a piece of property than the client knows about. And that is because the salesman fails to tell him. Of course, by doing all of those things and keeping it a secret, he'll end up with a frustrated client. The client will react bitterly, 'My home is still on the market. What a no-good bum!' " Even when the house sells the client complains, "That realtor made a twenty-thousand-dollar commission for selling my home and he didn't do a thing to deserve it." It is a shame when a salesperson, does, in fact, do a good job but keeps it a secret. The customer is in the dark, and the salesperson receives neither repeat orders nor referrals; instead of creating goodwill, the opposite occurs.

The lesson here is to give exceptional service and let your customers know about it. Do not be bashful about selling yourself. Let the world know you for your exceptional service.

Customers Really Do Appreciate Exceptional Service

How much are Americans willing to pay for good service? A lot.

Who would have thought that Federal Express, by guaranteeing overnight delivery, could charge such a premium? After all, the U.S. Postal Service delivers a one-ounce letter for twenty-five cents, and delivery to any point in the contiguous states takes one to three days. However, by guaranteeing delivery within twenty-four hours, Federal Express charges eleven dollars when the customer drops off a letter at one of its locations, or fourteen dollars if it's picked up. Depending upon the customer's preference, that is a premium of 4,400 to 5,600 percent! Evidently, Americans do place a high value on good service.

Honda Motor Company's senior vice president of automobile operations, Tom Elliott, says: "Our research shows that the price of a car is not the most important reason why people buy from a particular dealer—outstanding service is. The average customer will pay more to a dealer from whom he or she has received good service in the past. Of course, there is a point where a particular dealer can price himself out of the ballpark, no matter how good the service is."

People do value exceptional service, and when you give it, they will continue to do business with you. What's more, they will go out of their way to refer prospects to you. They value you as their salesperson, and they want you to succeed. So, in the long run, providing outstanding service is not an option, it is essential. In determining the success of your sales career, it must be measured in terms of longevity, not on one-time orders. In this respect, hardball selling is synonymous with building a valuable block of customers by serving them and then owning them.

11

The Hardball Code of Conduct

It is certain that the unconventional selling doctrine advocated in this book will not be universally accepted. Hardball selling will be criticized, particularly by the uninformed. To adhere to hardball selling principles, you must have conviction and tenacity.

It is important for you to realize there are no magic success formulas that work all the time, and certainly this is no exception. Hardball selling is not an exact science; it does not work every time. Accordingly, there will be discouraging moments that tempt you to disregard it and go back to your old ways of selling. However, hardball selling will produce desirable results; in the long run you will realize substantial increases in your earnings. As an added bonus, you will do so with a minimum of stress and grief.

Because hardball selling is a combination of technique and philosophy, a code of conduct is included herein. I recommend that you review it regularly, and above all, apply it with every customer.

- *Your integrity is your most valuable asset.* Your word is your bond. Avoid putting yourself in a position where your integrity is in question. Never misrepresent even what may seem like the slightest fact. Because your integrity is your most valuable asset, it can never be compromised. Your reputation is always on the line, and, while it takes years to establish a good one, you can lose it overnight. Since you use high-pressure tactics, it is probable that you will be more carefully scrutinized than other salespeople. Welcome it. You have nothing to hide, and what they find out about you will only serve to benefit you.

- *Be a follow-through person.* Whatever you say you will do, you must do. This is a simple rule, yet it is a rare individual who abides by it. If you are dependable, people will rely on you. They will also know what to expect because there will be no surprises. Generally, customers feel comfortable doing business with salespeople when they can be confident about what they're getting.

- *Be prepared.* Being knowledgeable about your profession provides you with complete confidence and enables you to speak with authority and conviction. Customers respect expertise, so do your homework and be an expert. It is unprofessional to be unprepared; under no circumstances is it acceptable.

- *Tackle problems head-on.* You must immediately meet all obstacles head-on. The more time that lapses in contacting a customer with a problem or complaint, the less likely it will be resolved. Even when a problem cannot be adequately resolved, a prompt response is valued and helps establish a long-term relationship.

- *Admit when you have erred.* When you are wrong, admit it promptly and without reservation. Whenever possible, inform your customer about your mistake before he brings it to your attention. It is far better if you are the one to reveal your blunder—it builds credibility.

- *Never hide behind company policy.* Saying "It's against company policy" is likely to antagonize people. From a customer's viewpoint, simply because a company arbitrarily establishes a policy does not make it a good one. If a policy exists, you must never state it without providing a good explanation.

- *Avoid being stereotyped.* Most people stereotype salespeople, but unfortunately, in a negative way. To avoid being stereotyped, you should be conservative in your dress, jewelry, hairstyle, makeup, etc. Also avoid other behavior patterns such as using overworked expressions and buzz words. For example, never use such phrases as "To be perfectly honest with you," "Now this is the truth," or "Trust me." While these trite expressions are nothing more than idle comments, they have dishonest connotations. Furthermore, always look directly into someone's eyes; some people mistrust salespeople who avoid eye contact (although it's likely to be an indication of shyness rather than a lack of integrity). People have misconceptions, and, although they may be unfounded, you must take them seriously.

- *Avoid obvious bad habits and controversial behavior.* Gum chewing, smoking, and drinking should never occur in the presence of your customers during official business hours—even when the customer indulges and invites you to join him. Since he is the customer, he has more liberties than you. If nothing else, abstinence demonstrates good discipline.

- *Be single-minded.* "The secret of success is constancy to purpose," said Benjamin Disraeli. With each presentation, your single purpose for being there is to close the sale. Once the sale is made your single purpose is service. This single-minded objective provides you with focused direction that blocks out distractions and keeps you on track at all times.

- *Selling and servicing are synonymous.* You must never separate selling and servicing. Providing outstanding service is a vital part of your job description. Serving customers is equally important to closing sales.

- *Always strive for excellence.* Your ultimate success will be determined by your performance. You must constantly strive to excel in every endeavor of your work. When you achieve across-the-board excellence, success is imminent.

- *Be totally committed to hardball selling.* You cannot take parts of this book piecemeal and use only what seems appropriate for you. You must accept the book in its entirety. If you delete certain segments, the rest, out of context, will result in a fruitless effort. There is no room for compromise. A total commitment to hardball selling is essential.

12

Selling Abroad

By applying the hardball concepts of Chapters One through Eleven, you can make your closing ratio improve substantially. I feel comfortable making this statement, but I must qualify it: I advise you, when selling abroad, to apply any hardball selling techniques with extreme caution because *what works here in America won't necessarily work in places such as West Germany, Japan, Israel, and Saudia Arabia.* In fact, what I have told you could even backfire and lose sales for you in many foreign countries.

The wave of the future calls for a worldwide marketplace. Those who fail to think globally are doomed to go the way of the dinosaur. No longer can a salesperson think in terms of territories limited to city, county, or state boundaries. I believe that for America to enter the twenty-first century as an economic leader, her legions of salespeople must sell successfully to a world market.

Gearing Americans to enter a world marketplace, however, is no easy task. Selling abroad demands a set of skills different from those required domestically, skills based on a clear understanding of the customs and business practices of individual countries. Before selling abroad, you must do your homework to make the necessary cultural adjustments required in each specific land. We must shed our "ugly American" image, an image based on our ignorance and disregard of the traditions and conventions of host nations. We have entered a new era in which Americans no longer can insist on others' "doing it our way," without concern for whether we are disliked or merely tolerated by the rest of the world. Today's American salesperson must view himself or herself as a self-proclaimed goodwill ambassador.

It probably would take a volume of books to furnish the know-how for selling in each marketplace in the world. With this in mind, I have tried in this single chapter simply to create an awareness of the importance of being properly prepared when selling outside the United States. Anyone who tries to enter a foreign market without knowing the lay of the land is bound to miss the mark, regardless of sales background or past performances. Let me emphasize that *no one* can succeed in an alien environment without knowing the rules. Here's just a handful of cultural differences that can become pitfalls if a salesperson is ignorant of them, even if that person is acting in good faith:

- In Australia, to say one is "full" following a meal means one is drunk. If the wording is changed to "stuffed," the meaning has sexual overtones.

- In Greece, the American okay sign (thumb and forefinger touching in a circle) is an obscene gesture.

- In Israel, the Sabbath begins at sundown Friday and ends at sundown Saturday. It is offensive to suggest conducting business within this period.

- It is rude to inquire about an Arab's wife and family if you have not met them. Furthermore, never use your left hand for holding, offering, or receiving anything from an Arab. The left hand is used for handling toilet paper. If you write with your left hand, you must apologize for doing so.

- When visiting England, Scotland, or Wales, avoid using the word *England* or *English* in reference to Great Britain as a whole. Everyone will be pleased if you use the word *British.* Also remember that you may smoke after the toast to Her Majesty's health, but never before.

- In Egypt, don't expect promptness at a business meeting.

- In Thailand, it is an insult to pat anyone, even a child, on the head.

- While Americans take pride in being outspoken and forthright, the Greeks deplore it, considering it as a lack of finesse. And while Americans conduct business meetings and delegate the paperwork to subordinates, the Greeks consider this behavior as deceptive. Instead, they insist on working out the details in front of all parties, no matter how long the meeting takes.

- In India, cows are sacred, so never give a gift made of cowhide.

- Brazilians are nonstop talkers. They make constant physical contact with other people, and continually say "no" during the course of a conversation, which doesn't necessarily translate into a lack of interest, but instead into "perhaps" or "let's discuss it further."

- During the course of a business meeting, it is common for the Japanese to listen with their eyes closed, and they are known for taking long pauses to reflect during a conversation. Furthermore, the Japanese don't like confrontations, so they say *"hai"* continuously during business discussions. Although *hai* means "yes," sometimes it just tells the other party that "I am listening" and "I understand what you say." When a Japanese says, *"Kangae sasete kudasai"* ("Let me think about it"), it almost always means no. And when he says, *"Ei doryoku shimasu"* ("We shall make every attempt"), you can expect a slow-motion response. While Americans like yes and no answers, the Japanese don't like either; they prefer the gray areas.

- Refer to the country as the Soviet Union, not Russia.

- Blowing your nose in front of others is considered bad manners in South Korea.

- Tipping rules can leave you even more confused. In Europe, you're expected to tip just about everything that moves, from the waiter to the movie usher to public bathroom attendants. In a restaurant, the average gratuity is 10 to 15 percent, and don't assume that just because it's covered in the check you're off the hook. French waiters usually expect a few francs more. Most Asians reject the whole practice and will chase you down the street to return a tip. In Japan, tipping is associated with begging, and practically nobody, including bellhops, accepts tips.

Rather than trying to cite the proper behavior in every country, the rest of this chapter will focus on selling in Japan.

I have selected Japan for two reasons: First, no other country's economic power so strongly influences the rest of the world. Second, our two nation's cultures are strikingly different. When one first arrives in Tokyo, the city looks so Americanized that one can be initially fooled into believing our two countries are quite alike. They're not. The message you will read about Japan is also applicable when selling in other places outside the United States.

Are Cultural Barriers Conquerable?

Although some cultural barriers seem insurmountable, it is possible to sell effectively in any country. Unfortunately, the differences sometimes seem such great obstacles that many salespeople automatically shy away from trying to tackle them. To see that it is possible, observe how it worked in reverse when Japan entered the U.S. marketplace.

When Japan first began selling her wares in America in the 1950s, the merchandise was limited to cheap trinkets, toys, and Madame Butterfly–type dolls. Nobody made any bones about it: "Made in Japan" stood for shoddy quality. The Japanese had to overcome many complicated legal barriers, and with Americans still harboring hostility toward Japan for the bombing of Pearl Harbor, there was considerable racial prejudice that led to ethnic slurs. And then there was the language barrier.

Putting hindsight aside, what odds would you have given to the Japanese that they would succeed? It's no wonder Secretary of State John Foster Dulles suggested to Prime Minister Yoshida that Japan's export strategy and energy should be directed at Southeast Asia rather than being wasted in America. Dulles bluntly stated that the Japanese didn't make what Americans wanted, nor was it possible for them to overcome the cultural and language barriers in order to meet

America's competitive dominance head on. Isn't it interesting how many Americans perceive today's Japanese market in a similar vein?

A good example of one leading Japanese company that misjudged the U.S. market in the fifties was Honda when it first came to the United States in 1959 to peddle motorcycles. The company failed to realize that because the United States had such vast open spaces and wide roads, motorcycles would be driven at greater speeds and for longer distances than in Japan. Consequently, the first models shipped to America malfunctioned; only after Honda engineers in Tokyo redesigned the head gasket and clutch spring, and conducted road tests, was the company, a year later, able to come out with a motorcycle that would serve the needs of the American consumer. With its international philosophy of manufacturing products to fit the needs of each specific marketplace, Honda today has more than a 50 percent share of the world motorcycle market.

Honda and other Japanese companies succeeded in our marketplace while operating under severe handicaps, and we can do the same in Japan. In comparison, our obstacles are not nearly as burdensome as what the Japanese encountered, because, although America's economy has fallen a notch or two, we are still a world leader in numerous industries. Let us remember that we are blessed with a wealth of natural resources. In contrast, Japan was a struggling, war-torn nation. We also enjoy the advantage of studying how the Japanese overcame cultural differences in our country. Now it's our turn to duplicate that success.

Understanding Why Cultural Differences Exist

A brief study of a nation's history is a fine way to uncover cultural differences. In the case of Japan and the United States, one quick way to do so is to understand the Japanese word *mottainai*, which means "all things are precious and to waste is a sin." To understand this word, observe the striking contrast between the two nations in land surface area. Japan is a country of limited resources, while the United States is a land of plenty. Americans live in a disposable society.

Japan's population of 122 million, compared to our 240 million, live in an area the size of California, but its terrain is jagged and mountainous, so only 17 percent of the land is habitable. Its population density of 318 people per square kilometer is fifteen times greater than ours, and 3.5 times that of China. In the early 1600s, Japan's population density had already soared to nearly twice that of the present-day United States. To put it still another way, if we had the same amount of land as Japan but our present density, there would be only 15.5 million citizens of this country. What this boils down to is that a nation with more than half our population lives on a land surface about one twenty-fifth of ours.

With virtually no natural resources, Japan imports 83 percent of its energy, in contrast to 59 percent for France and 9.6 percent for the United States. Japan is 100 percent dependent on imports for aluminum, iron ore, and nickel, 95 percent dependent for copper, and more than 92 percent dependent for natural gas. The Japanese people understand the scarcity of the most precious resource—food. Almost everyone over the age of fifty—40 percent of the population—remembers the severe food shortages that accompanied World War II and its aftermath, when many ate grasshoppers and boiled grass to survive. Japan's farmers produce barely enough to feed 50 percent of its people, so if imports were cut off, the Japanese would suffer as they did during the war. With such vast shortages in land and natural resources, the Japanese have good reason to think, live, and work differently. Only when one realizes the country's deficiencies can one understand why certain aspects of Japanese behavior must differ from ours in America. As recently as the last century, the American pioneer headed west, discovering a huge virgin territory on which farms and ranches could be built, often miles from the nearest neighbor. These early settlers were passionately independent, an American characteristic even today, and a trait that is directly opposed to the Japanese group-oriented philosophy, which seeks harmony. With the diverse backgrounds of the two peoples, it is no wonder that personality characteristics differ. Americans are aggressive and argumentative; Japanese are passive and will go to extremes to avoid conflict.

The above descriptions are generalizations, and it should be remembered that every human being is unique. It is important to avoid stereotyping. But marked cultural differences between our countries do exist, with each difference having a logical explanation.

Recognizing differences and why they exist sometimes is necessary to understand the reasons why some products popular in America would not be well received in other places. The lack of space in Japan could be the cause, for example, for the poor sales of recreational vehicles and lawn mowers. And in a land where resources are scarce, it is logical that a strong emphasis would be placed on quality goods that last longer.

Understanding the limited resources and land also helps explain the long-term thinking of the Japanese people, a characteristic that one must clearly comprehend to engage in business in Japan successfully. For example, the average Japanese citizen puts about 20 percent of his or her annual disposable income into savings. Not only does this figure rank as the highest rate of personal savings in any major nation, it is nearly four times what the average American saves. Also compare the Japanese illiteracy rate, at less than 2 percent, to the 20 percent rate in the United States. And take a look at the large amount of money put into research and development in Japan. Honda, for example, invests 5 percent of its annual earnings in R&D, compared to the U.S. automotive industry average of 3.5 percent and the American business average of 1.5 percent.

Yet another striking contrast is American industries' concern for short-term profits versus Japanese industries' commitment to long-term gains. Corporate America keeps score on a three-month basis with progress reports. While corporate Japan does issue quarterly reports, its concentration is on market share and long-term results. Unlike American stockholders, Japanese investors don't meddle in management, nor do they press for short-term profitability and cost-cutting measures.

What do high savings, an emphasis on education, a commitment to R&D, and a commitment to long-term gains mean? They tell us that the Japanese people have a deep concern for the future. The Japanese are willing to make sacrifices today for a better tomorrow.

From a salesperson's point of view, there is another message that should be heard. Japanese companies are interested in establishing long-term relationships with those they conduct business with. For this reason the lowest bidder doesn't necessarily win the contract. Product quality, delivery schedules, and customer satisfaction are vital considerations. Knowing this, a salesperson would be wise to base his initial sales presentation to a Japanese firm on the strength of the organization that he represents. In this respect, he should emphasize that his company has depth in both management and resources—in other words, it will perform as promised for many years to come.

A Brief Lesson in Japanese Business Etiquette

As you know, customs differ from region to region, even within this country, so it should come as no surprise that customs are not the same halfway around the world. What is considered in good or bad taste in the United States may be viewed differently in Japan.

I am sure you would never knowingly insult a prospective customer in Japan. But you may do so unintentionally, and your inappropriate behavior could cause you to lose a sale. Again, my intention is merely to create an awareness that a certain etiquette must be followed, but keep in mind that it isn't possible for me to teach a complete course on the subject within the confines of this chapter. You'll have to do additional reading to learn the details. What I will do, however, is pass on to you twenty-four tips that I think will help you in your business dealings with the Japanese:

- Introductions to businesspeople are more important in Japan than they are in this country. Consequently, cold calls are considerably more difficult. Preferably, you should have a third party call or write to the prospect on your behalf to arrange your first meeting.

- There are several who's who—type books in Japan that list business people who hold titles above the section chief level. By doing your homework, you can learn about a potential customer's religion, education, special interests, hobbies, names of family members, and so on. And by writing to Dodwell Marketing Consultants, C.P.O. Box 257, Tokyo, Japan, you can obtain a copy of *Dodwell International,* a book that lists what companies are integrated into other Japanese companies. This knowledge can be valuable for networking in Japan.

- Not only should you be on time for business appointments, I recommend that you arrive ten minutes early. Throughout my career, I made it a practice always to put a 110 percent effort into everything I did. Knowing that the Japanese admire hard work, you won't score points with them if you show any sign of laziness. It's an understatement to say that laziness is not their style.

- To break the ice properly at an initial business meeting, some brief small talk is appropriate. Subjects should be limited to general topics such as the weather, golf, or baseball. For obvious reasons, avoid discussing politics. While in the United States getting right down to business is admired, it is considered overly aggressive in Japan.

- The Japanese express themselves in language that is vague and ambiguous. For example, when asking about a company's yearly sales, a Japanese who has just reviewed the company's annual report and knows the number is exactly $8.4 billion is likely to reply, "Oh, a few billion." To give a precise answer is considered impertinent and boastful.

- When a Japanese nods his head while listening, he isn't necessarily agreeing with what you say, but politely acknowledging that he understands what you have said.

- The Japanese work hard at avoiding confrontations. While Americans say, "The squeaking wheel gets the grease," the Japanese say, "The pheasant would not be shot but for its cry."

- During a telephone conversation, you should either say *"hai"* or make grunting sounds to inform a Japanese that you follow what has been said.

- It is common for long pauses to occur during the course of a business meeting while a Japanese thinks through his position before speaking. During these periods, be careful not to interrupt. Unlike Americans, the Japanese don't think silence is a flaw in a conversation. In an ordinary conversation among Americans, the usual response time is a few tenths of a second, so a five- to ten-second delay can be puzzling. And sometimes, the silence continues for as long as twenty to twenty-five seconds during a business meeting with a group of Japanese executives. Not a word is spoken, and all keep their eyes lowered with their hands folded on the table.

- Japanese business people rarely display emotion, and therefore it is difficult to judge their interest. Typically, their facial expressions are deadpan; during a first meeting, it is unusual for them to smile. They are more likely to communicate through body language. For instance, when a Japanese businessman keeps changing his position in his chair, crossing and uncrossing his legs, or shifting from side to side, he is probably signaling his boredom. Body language is often used purposefully to show lack of interest.

- While American salespeople are advised to look others squarely in the eye, eye contact is not interpreted as a sign of honesty in Japan. In fact, too much eye contact is considered impolite. A rule of thumb is to limit your eye contact to five seconds. A Japanese employee might lower his head out of respect when addressing his or her manager; the higher the rank within an organization, the less eye contact there is likely to be with a superior.

- Unlike the Arabs, who have small zones of personal space (an Arab feels uncomfortable if he can't smell your breath), the Japanese feel that a person standing too close is intrusive and overly aggressive. A reserved people, they keep a greater distance from others than do Americans. Knowing this, you should minimize physical contact. I've heard horror stories about how an American gave a good-ol'-boy backslap to a Japanese and thus blew a multimillion-dollar deal!

- In Japan, spouses are not included in business-related entertainment such as dining out or after-hours cocktails.

- By our present standards, Japan is a male-chauvinist society. For example, women walk behind men, even when exiting elevators. And, among other differences, the men order their meals first in restaurants.

- There is a Japanese custom that dictates where a guest is seated in a room. As a gesture of humbleness, the host will sit closest to the door, which is considered the least desirable place. Proper etiquette seats the guest on the side of the room, furthest from the door. As a general rule, the guest will have the best view in the room, facing a window or a beautiful painting. Foreign visitors often enter a room and unknowingly plop themselves in the host's seat, causing their host to feel uncomfortable.

- During the course of a business meeting, somebody may enter the room unannounced and take a seat in the back of the room without saying a word. In all likelihood, this individual is a top executive, the most senior manager in the group. You can be sure that the lower-ranking people will not arrive late. Not wanting to interrupt the meeting, this person may remain silent, but be assured that his opinion makes a difference. I suggest that you introduce yourself to him and treat him with the utmost respect.

- As a sign of humility, Japanese will downplay themselves during the course of a conversation. For instance, they might apologize for speaking English so poorly. An American might unwittingly ignore the remark, but the proper response would be, "You speak very well." In turn, a Japanese would answer, "No, no, it is not good." Once more, the reply should be, "Yes, you must have studied quite a bit of English." On the other hand, an American told that his Japanese is good often will say, "Thank you," even though he speaks only a handful of words. In Japan, this response is considered arrogant and in poor taste. (The Japanese study English for several years and know our language considerably better than we know theirs. Yet they are the ones who deny their fluency in our tongue.) You can be certain that the Japanese will not accept other compliments either.

- It is considered in poor taste to knock a competitor. If you think some comparative information is essential, express the weaknesses of your competition by emphasizing your strengths. For example, rather than saying, "XYZ Company has horrendous problems internally," you should say, "I would like to tell you something about how our organization has made an extra effort to deal with this," or "I'd like to point out an important aspect of my company that I think might interest you. I feel that it distinguishes our organization from others." This approach is more subtle, but the Japanese will pick up on it.

- You should avoid making frequent or pointed references to contractual obligations. Their attorneys are not nearly as involved in business matters as American attorneys, and the Japanese prefer not to make an issue out of the fine print in a written agreement. Furthermore, they don't like to quote it. They are more concerned with the bond that has been formed between the two parties than with how a responsibility to perform is mandatory according to the written agreement. I am not suggesting, however, that the Japanese do not honor the contents of a contract. They simply prefer not to discuss this subject with business associates.

- The Japanese have a greater interest in market share than in profits. To say, "This deal will generate millions of dollars in profits" is less appealing than "This can give your company an x percent increase in market share."

- Discussing money matters is in poor taste. The Japanese don't like to discuss finances with you, so don't talk about how much things cost, such as last night's dinner, a round of golf, or the money your deal made for them. And once a deal is made, leave the price to go-betweens or lower-echelon managers.

- If you receive a price that you feel is unreasonable, don't automatically reject it or strongly protest. To do so would be insulting. Instead, act as though you will consider it. Then explain that while you would like to meet this price, you regret that is not possible. By doing so, you leave the door open for negotiations.

- No one practices the art of gift giving more enthusiastically than the Japanese. Twice a year, in December (*Oseibo*) and July (*Ochugen*), they exchange gifts with their business contacts, either to express appreciation or to repay an obligation. Gift wrapping is associated with many traditions and symbolic gestures in Japan, including matters of how the paper is folded, the choice of the cord, and the style in which it is knotted. The Japanese are most apt to use colored wrapping paper and fabric. In the ancient tradition, a wrapped gift is then bound up in a silk scarf (a *furoshiki*), which is the final wrapping. When a Japanese presents you with a gift, the nice thing to do is express your thanks and make a small bow in appreciation. It is considered rude for an executive traveling on business to surprise a Japanese colleague with a gift. It will make him lose face, and he will feel compelled immediately to buy a return gift. Let him be the first to give the gift when you are in his country. If you reciprocate, your gift should be slightly less expensive than his. Give him something American. He will cherish a gift of art—a painting, weaving, sculpture, or ceramic piece by an American artist. The Japanese also appreciate ties (in somber colors), and scarves and handbags for the women, particularly if they have trendy designers' names attached. And, of course, liquor is a welcome gift. The major department stores in Tokyo, such as Takashimaya and Mitsukoshi, have large catalogs listing suggested items for business gifts. You can request these stores to deliver a gift to somebody on a specified date and time.

- Although your initial order from a Japanese firm might be small, don't be discouraged. The Japanese like to test the waters. If you maintain good communications and provide quality goods, dependable delivery, and outstanding service, you will build a long-term relationship and larger orders will follow.

Dealing with the Language Barrier

Of all the barriers, language is the most obvious. While it may not be possible or practical for you to learn to speak Japanese in preparation for a trip to Japan, the more you know, the better off you'll be. As a matter of courtesy, you should at least make an attempt to learn a few words, such as:

English	Japanese
Good morning	Ohayo gozaimasu
Good afternoon	Konnichiwa
Good evening	Kombanwa
Good night	Oyasumi nasai
Good-bye	Sayonara
How do you do?	Hajime-mashite
How are you?	Ogenki desuka?
Mr. (Mrs., Miss) Tanaka	Tanaka-san
Please	Do-o-zo
Thank you	Arigato gozaimasu
Excuse me	Gomen nasai; Shitsurei shimasu
A moment, please	Chotto matte kudasai
You're welcome	Do itashi-mashite

This severely limited vocabulary will not enable you to converse with anyone, but memorizing it does show that you cared enough to take the time to learn a few words of Japanese. It's a shame, but many Americans still seem to think English is a universal language of business, so "it isn't necessary to speak another language because all educated foreigners speak ours." As Henry Ferguson, one of the nation's leading experts on importing and exporting, states in his book *Tomorrow's Global Executive,* "It's a myth that continues to blind American businesspersons to the realities of business and bedevil their chances of success. It is badly false. With arrogance of this nature, it is no wonder our trade deficit is so high."

I think one way America can begin to compete more effectively is by practicing what other countries are doing, and that is to send large numbers of our youth abroad to learn foreign languages and cultures. Note, for example, that barely eight hundred U.S. citizens are studying at Japanese universities. But the National Science Foundation says that some thirteen thousand Japanese are studying at U.S. universities. I don't think putting tariffs on imported goods is a long-term solution to competing in a world marketplace. Instead, Americans must do what the Japanese have done in order to succeed in our country: learn our culture and communicate in our language. In my opinion, this is no longer an option, but a necessity.

Fortunately, most Japanese businesspeople speak enough English to enable them to converse with you, but keep in mind that it is not their native tongue. Here are five basic tips to keep in mind: (1) Speak at a slower rate than usual. (2) Even though a Japanese may speak English, he might not clearly understand it. Don't assume that because he keeps nodding everything you say is registering. (3) Avoid local expressions (it's even difficult for New Englanders, for example, to understand many of the words used by Texans, so don't expect foreigners to "dig" your local slang). They won't understand regional expressions or terms that do not translate literally. With this in mind, don't use sayings such as "It's a new ball game," "raining cats and dogs," "as clear as mud," and "don't make waves." (4) Limit your joke telling to wholesome and easily understood punchlines. The Japanese have a different sense of humor from ours. (5) During a business meeting, incorporate the use of graphics and overhead slides into your presentation.

While a Japanese may feel comfortable speaking English during a social conversation, the same executive will probably have a skilled interpreter on hand during an important business discussion. By the same token, it would be foolish for you to attend a business meeting without a qualified interpreter. It's recommended that you spend several hours briefing this person on the background of your industry, company, and product. Be sure to let the interpreter know what you really want to say. And equally as vital as speaking the language is understanding the culture. For instance, it would be a mistake to have a Japanese-speaking American, who has not lived in Japan for several years, serve in this capacity. Many Japanese believe they can communicate with each other largely without using words. They do so by *haragei*, or what we could call "belly language." Through *haragei*, the Japanese can convey their messages through casual glances, occasional grunts, and meaningful silences. Foreigners, no matter how fluent in Japanese, rarely pick up on this silent language.

Be Prepared!

Over the years, I have seen many salespeople fall flat on their faces because they underestimated the differences in foreign markets and consequently failed to make alterations in their sales presentations. This does not mean that I am suggesting you abandon the hardball selling philosophy, because, for the most part, it works universally, with some adjustments. However, each country is unique and presents a different set of challenges. By doing your homework in advance, you will most likely succeed, because, all things being equal, people around the world are still people.

So, as I have emphasized throughout this book, being properly prepared is a strength on which a hardball salesperson capitalizes. This is particularly applicable when selling abroad. Under no circumstances should you walk in cold without a clear understanding of a particular country's culture. To do so is not only unprofessional, it is certain to be a waste of time and money.

CHAPTER
13

A Final Message

Many will consider *Hardball*'s message bold and controversial. It is a challenge to you, the reader, to dare to be different. Its unconventional content will certainly attract the attention of every salesperson. Yet, I suspect only a small percentage of readers will become hardball advocates. I base this on the fact that most people resist change; in particular, they resist radical change. This resistance stems from the anxiety of risk-taking, which is not unlike the fear felt by the procrastinating prospect discussed in this book.

However, before you rule out accepting change, I urge you to consider the rewards of hardball selling. For instance, every top salesperson knows when to apply high-pressure selling, and does so without the least hesitation. If you know a supersalesperson who does not, I would like to meet this unique individual. You have a choice: You can remain satisfied with the status quo, or you can accept the doctrine of hardball selling. By choosing hardball selling, you are taking control of your future.